Historic Wa

South and West Yorkshire

C000180534

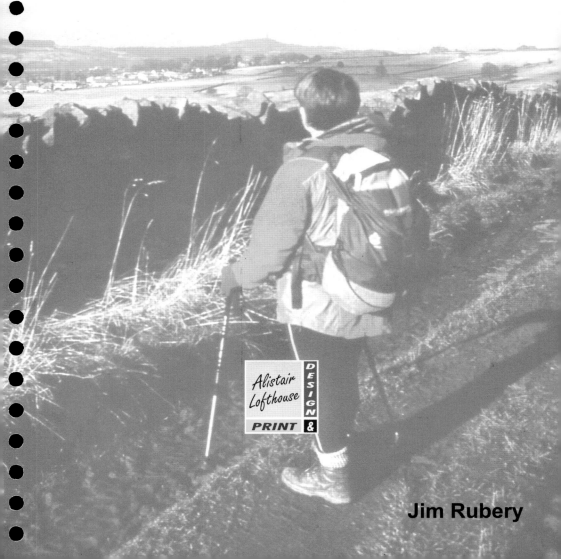

Alistair Lofthouse DESIGN & PRINT

Jim Rubery

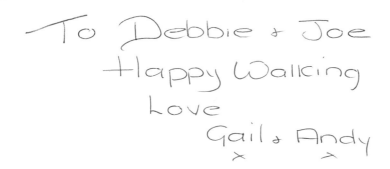

To Debbie & Joe
Happy Walking
Love
Gail & Andy
x

© Jim Rubery 2006

Colour photographs and drawings: Jim Rubery

Printed and Published by:
ALD Design & Print
279 Sharrow Vale Road
Sheffield, S11 8ZF

Telephone 0114 2679402
email a.lofthouse@btinternet.com

ISBN 1-901587-43-6

First published July 2006

Other titles in the series

8 Walks around the Monsal Trail	Jim Rubery	ISBN 1-901587-39-8
Historical Walks of West & South Yorkshire	Jim Rubery	ISBN 1-901587-43-6
Then & Now - The Monsal Trail	Alistair Lofthouse	ISBN 1-901587-31-2

Contents

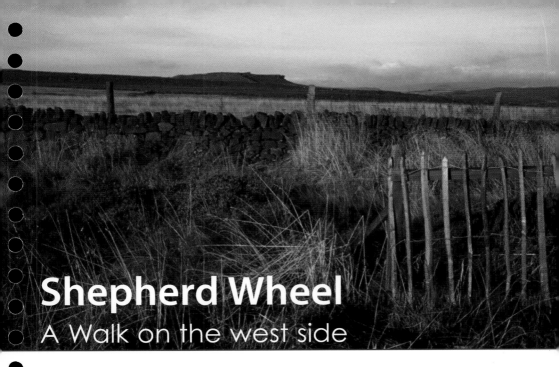

Shepherd Wheel
A Walk on the west side

Endcliffe Park - Shepherd Wheel - Porter Clough - Ringinglow - Houndkirk Moor - Fox House

Introduction

The Pennine Hills that fringe the industrial towns and cities of northern England have for centuries provided a haven of peace, relaxation and fresh air, away from the smoke, dirt and noise of the factories. This is particularly so in Sheffield, home to George Ward, 'king of ramblers', who spent much of his life pioneering for increased public access to our hills and countryside. This fine, linear walk follows one of many 'green arteries' that run from deep within the city to the heather clad moors that grace its western fringe and one that has been used by thousands of escapees who 'may be workslaves on Monday, but are free men on Sunday'.

Points of interest

Hunter's Bar was the last of the toll bars to be used in Sheffield and took the last of its fees on 31st October 1884. Shepherd Wheel is a superb survivor of a water powered grinding hull, used for grinding cutlery. Ringinglow Round House was built as a toll house but is now a private dwelling. Fox House Inn was once an important coaching inn set high on the moors between Derbyshire and Yorkshire.

Information

Distance & time:	6 miles (10.5km) 3hrs. approx.
Start & finish:	Hunter's Bar, Sheffield on A625. Grid Ref: 332857.
Maps:	OS Explorer 278 Sheffield & Barnsley.
Parking:	Roadside parking around Hunter's Bar. Note any restrictions.
Public Transport:	Services from City to Hunters Bar: 50, 59, 65, 240, 250, 272. From Fox House to City: 65, 240. 272. Tel: 01709 515151
Refreshments:	Cafes in parks, pubs at Ringinglow & Fox House.
Tourist Information:	Peace Gardens, Sheffield, S1 2HH. Tel: 0114 2734672
Shepherd Wheel:	Free admission but very restricted opening. Groups can be pre-booked. Tel: 0114 2367731

• Ringinglow's Round House   • Queen Victoria in Endcliffe Park

Directions

1. From Hunters Bar roundabout on the A625, enter Endcliffe Park and follow the broad, surfaced footpath past the statue of Queen Victoria, now heavily shrouded by a large Copper Beech tree, and on to the Park Cafe.

Sheffield is well endowed with parks and open spaces, many of which once formed the gardens and estates of large halls and houses. Endcliffe Park is a pleasing blend of large grassy areas and mature woodland that sits astride the tiny River Porter, a waterway that has been a slave to steel and is commonly referred to as the Porter Brook.

At a 'Y' fork just beyond the cafe bear right over the brook to reach Holme Wheel Dam, the first of seven dams along the valley.

In the early days of Sheffield's famous cutlery industry, and even up to the early 1900's, water power was relied upon for most of the grinding and hammering processes. In 1604, 28 water wheels were recorded on the streams and rivers around Sheffield, by 1770 the number had risen to 133 with 15 sited along the River Porter. Dams were built on or alongside the streams and rivers so that a good head of water could be tapped for turning the wheels and also to ensure a power supply in times of drought.

Just beyond the dam cross the brook again and continue alongside it, passing Nether Spur-Gear Wheel Dam on the left, to reach Rustlings Road.

2. Cross with care then go right for a few yards before turning left into Bingham Park.

The steep, grassy slopes to the left provide excellent sledgeing for local youngsters (and many adults too) in the winter and during spring, swathes of yellow daffodils cloak the park.

A short way into the park and a little to the right lies Ibbotson Wheel Dam, home to an extensive population of well fed waterfowl. Just beyond here and shaded by mature trees is the splendid Shepherd Wheel.

This is the only intact survivor of 20 water powered sites that once stood alongside the Porter Brook. It is a fine example of how Sheffield's renowned metal-working skills developed along the waterways that flow from the moors on the western edge of the city. It consists of two grinding 'hulls' or workshops where cutlery was produced and both are in a remarkable state of preservation. Unfortunately, the 18ft. diameter, overshot water-wheel that powers the mill has not been in operation for over two years due to a number of the wooden 'buckets' being rotten. Records show that a water mill has stood here since 1584 but its present name comes from a Mr. Shepherd who rented the property in the late 1700's.

Continue through the park, crossing Highcliffe Road into Whiteley Woods where the footpath runs parallel to the brook.

3. Cross Whiteley Wood Road, taking the left-hand footpath through the woods, with the brook now down to the right.

The bed of the brook is stained deep reddish-brown in places where iron deposits have been leached out from the surrounding rocks and soils. The reason why the iron and steel industry developed around Sheffield is due to a rich supply of iron ore in the surrounding hills, an abundance of woodland to provide charcoal for smelting, fast flowing streams for power and millstone grit from which the grindstones could be cut, many of which now lie abandoned and unused on the surrounding moors.

At a junction with Ivy Cottage Lane bear left, following the white railings round to Forge Dam Playground and Cafe, just beyond which and at a slightly higher level is Forge Dam, home to another flock of rotund ducks. Continue on a good stony footpath to Carr Bridge, cross the road and follow the 'Round Walk' footpath sign into the Mayfield Valley; regarded by many as the most beautiful on the western fringes of the city.

An intricate network of tracks and narrow lanes criss-cross the valley with its sloping fields, pockets of woodland and little hillside farms. The city planners have done a grand job here, resisting pressure from developers to build and so retaining the charms of this quiet, intimate valley.

Continue following signs for the 'Round Walk' which soon enters Porter Clough, a steep sided little ravine cut by the Porter Brook, where the path begins to rise steadily towards the moors. At a footpath sign just before the head of the clough, go left over the brook towards Ringinglow, pass through a car parking area, then bear left along Fulwood Road.

• The Little village of Ringinglow, the last outpost of South Yorkshire

4. At the 'T' junction in the little village of Ringinglow go left towards the Norfolk Arms, crossing into Sheephill Lane just before the pub and opposite Ringinglow Round House which, you will notice, is not round but octagonal.

Constructed in 1795 as the Barber Fields Cupola Tollhouse, this fine, multi-windowed building stands in a prominent position on the junction of three roads and at the point where the old turnpike road from Sheffield diverged; one branch going across the moors to Chapel-en-le Frith, the other to Fox House. To take advantage of the increasing amount of traffic crossing the moors at this point the Norfolk Arms, formerly the Ringinglow Inn, was built.

Just beyond the lovely house at Moor Cott, bear right onto Houndkirk Lane, a broad, stony track that once served as a main turnpike road into and out of Sheffield.

5. The character of the walk now changes dramatically from the shelter of the Mayfield Valley and Porter Clough to the vast, windswept expanses of Burbage and Houndkirk Moors and, as the track rises steadily alongside Lady Canning's Wood, fabulous views across South Yorkshire, Derbyshire and Nottinghamshire unfold. You are now in the Peak District National Park, the oldest and most visited of our National Parks.

There is a marked contrast between the green fields to the east where crops grow in lovingly tended soils and cattle graze lush pastures, and these high, heather moorlands where the wind always seems to blow and snow can lie for weeks on end. Only the hardy survive up here; the tough gritstone blackfaced sheep, the grouse, glossy bilberry and sturdy heather that turns these expanses into a sea of purple in late summer. It is also quite remarkable to think that only a short time ago you were in the busy suburbs of Yorkshire's most industrialised city and, with only a modicum of effort, you are now standing on some of the most exposed moorland in the Pennines.

It is this proximity to the Pennine Hills and the ease with which they can be accessed that gives Sheffield a landscape border that is unsurpassed by any other large British city.

The track rises to a little over 1400ft. before descending past Parson House Farm, now an Outdoor Pursuit Centre, to a junction with the A625. Turn right here to reach the Fox House Inn where buses will whisk you back into the heart of the city.

The Fox House stands at 1132ft. above sea level on the Yorkshire - Derbyshire border and was once an important coaching inn. It dates back to around 1773 when a two roomed shepherds cottage, built by a George Fox, stood on the site. In the past few years the inn has undergone major renovations and now boasts fine ales, good food and comfortable accommodation.

Wentworth Park & Elsecar

Wentworth - Elsecar - Street - Hoober - Low Stubbin - Nether Haugh - Wentworth Park

Introduction

This gentle walk, set in the rolling countryside between the industrial South Yorkshire towns of Barnsley and Rotherham, explores the magnificent Wentworth Woodhouse Estate, ancestral home of the Marquises of Rockingham and later Earls Fitzwilliam. Wentworth, a lovely estate village, is the starting point of the walk while Elsecar is a splendid example of an early coal and iron producing community, now steeped in historical interest.

Points of interest

Wentworth is a lovely estate village of mellow stone cottages with well tended gardens. Wentworth Woodhouse is a resplendent Palladian mansion which boasts the longest facade of any house in England. The Deer Park is a joy at any time of year and the area is littered with monuments and follies of all shapes and sizes. The conservation area and Heritage Centre at Elsecar is one of the most historically important in Yorkshire.

Information

Distance & time:	7 miles (11.25km) 3.5 hours, not including stops.
Start & finish:	Public car park, Main Street, Wentworth (next to Rockingham Arms).
Map:	OS Explorer 278 Sheffield & Barnsley.
Parking:	see start.
Public Transport:	Bus Services 44 & 227 from Barnsley & Rotherham. Tel: Travelline 01709 51 51 51.
Refreshments:	Pubs in Wentworth, Elsecar & Low Stubbin. Cafe at Wentworth & Elsecar Heritage Centre.
Tourist Information:	46 Eldon Street, Barnsley, South Yorks. S70 2JL. Tel: 01226 206757.
Elsecar Heritage Centre:	For opening times and further information contact: Elsecar Heritage Centre Tel: 01226 740203.

• An old traction engine at Elsecar Heritage Centre.

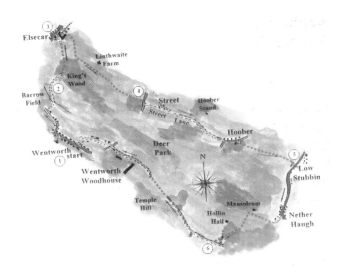

• Wentworth Woodhouse

Directions

1. From the car park, turn right along Main Street, passing attractive cottages with well tended gardens, Paradise Square being a particularly fine example.

Though established prior to the Norman Conquests, the village that we see here today was developed mainly as an estate village for Wentworth Woodhouse during the late 16th and 17th centuries. It is full of character with many interesting buildings including the Mechanics Institute, Ivy Cottage, reputed to be the oldest building in the village, Holy Trinity Church built between 1875 and 77 to replace the old church which stands nearby and dates from the 12th century. Besides two churches there are also two fine pubs, the George and Dragon and the Rockingham Arms. Servants, gardeners, gamekeepers and farm labourers were housed in the rows of cottages but in 1949, with the accidental death of the eighth Earl, great changes occurred. Massive death duties meant the house, along with many of its treasures were sold and many villagers lost their main source of income.

Just beyond the tree lined drive leading to the church, cross into Barrowfield Lane and follow this round to the left to reach the entrance to Wentworth Sawmills. Turn right here along a broad, concrete lane (footpath sign) that descends to cross Barrowfield Beck then swings round to the left before entering Low Wood.

2. At this point the track becomes unsurfaced as it swings round to the right towards King's Wood and alongside fields. Pass through a gate at the entrance to King's Wood, bear immediately left at a fork in the track and descend between fine mature trees where squirrels forage amongst the vegetation and songbirds flit through the canopy, to eventually exit the wood into a field. Walk straight across this, pass through a wall gap on the far side and continue ahead to a footpath junction by iron railings on the outskirts of Elsecar. Turn left through the railings and walk past old workshops in Forge Lane to reach the entrance to Elsecar Heritage Centre.

Elsecar was developed by the 4th, 5th and 6th Earls Fitzwilliam during the 18th and 19th centuries as a coal and iron producing community. They opened a number of collieries, iron works, numerous engineering workshops, a gasworks and a tar distillery; built the Elsecar branch of the Dearne & Dove canal and later opened their own private railway. The Fitwilliams had an unusually philanthropic approach to their workforce, providing them with housing and lodging that was well ahead of its time. The Miners' Lodging House in Fitzwilliam Street, now private apartments, is a particularly fine example.

Many of the buildings and monuments from this time have been lovingly and painstakingly restored, including 'The Earl Fitzwilliam', an 0-6-0 Avonside Saddleback locomotive that steams along a section of the old railway, making Elsecar Heritage Centre one of the most historically important in Yorkshire. It is now an enviable science, history and craft centre with many modern and traditional hand crafted items being made and sold from the old workshops.

3. After visiting, turn right out of the centre passing the Market Inn, turn right along Wath Road and at the end of the Heritage Centre go right again into Distillery Side and over the railway level crossing.

Over to the left at this point can be seen the Newcomen Beam Engine, the only engine of its type in the world which remains on its original site and as such is one of the most important industrial monuments in Britain. It was built in 1795 to a design by the Cornishman, Thomas Newcomen, in order to drain water from Elsecar New Mine and was used until 1928.

Keep right to join a footpath alongside a drystone wall, bear right at a fork in the track and continue across old, vegetated slag heaps to reach a cross footpath in front of a field. Turn left along this to the corner of King's Wood, keep ahead over a broad footpath for a few yards to a stile leading into a field and bear diagonally right across this, climbing steadily to a gap in a field fence. Continue in this direction first through, then alongside fields with Keppel's Column visible across the fields and woods to the right.

This 115 foot high column was designed by John Carr and built by the 2nd Marquis of Rockingham to commemorate the acquittal of his friend, Admiral Keppel, who was charged with cowardice in 1778.

4. Half way along Lee Wood the 'Needle's Eye' is passed, a pyramidal shaped structure that once stood astride one of the main approaches to the house.

This folly is believed to have been built by the 2nd Marquis so that he could win a wager that a coach could be driven 'through the eye of a needle'.

On reaching the road cross into Street Lane and follow this through the hamlet of Street where Hoober Stand soon comes into view above the trees to the left.

Another fine, pyramidal shaped monument, built between 1747 -9 to commemorate the suppression of the Jacobite rebellion. It crowns the highest ridge in the Wentworth area and the view from the upper cupola is quite splendid. It is open on Saturdays and Sundays, from 2 - 5pm, during August and September.

• Photos: 1.'The Earl Fitwilliam' at Rockingham Station. 2. Miners' Lodging House, Elsecar. 3. Hoober Stand.

At the road in Hoober, go left for 300 yards and on reaching Clematis cottage, cross to a stile and footpath immediately left of a private drive. Bear diagonally left through woodland, climb a stile on the far side then cross an open field before continuing round the left edge of fields to the road in Low Stubbin.

5. If refreshment is required, The Marquis inn lies along the road to the left, but to continue turn right along the road and follow it over the hill into Nether Haugh. Immediately beyond a left-hand bend, go right along a surfaced lane between cottages, follow it round to the right to join a grassy footpath that runs along the top edge of fields and past Mausoleum Plantation where the cupola of yet another of the Wentworth monuments can be seen jutting above the trees. At the far end of the field turn left to a stile at the bottom, bear half right across another field before descending alongside its far hedge to a footbridge and stile in the bottom corner. Once over, bear diagonally left through a broad grassy meadow, pass between trees bordering a track to a stile through a hedge on the far side, then cross the corner of another field to join a surfaced drive through the Wentworth Estate.

6. Turn right along this, cross a cattle grid and proceed through elegant parkland, landscaped in the 18th century by Humphrey Repton and where Red Deer browse beneath the boughs of the many fine trees and cattle graze the lush turf. On reaching the brow of Temple Hill, where a Doric Temple stands in a clearing over to the left, the magnificent 606 foot long, east facade of Wentworth Woodhouse comes into view; the longest house elevation in England.

This splendid building to which most 18th century architects have, at some time, been ascribed, is a posthumous symbol of the power and wealth of England's 18th century aristocracy. The estate was originally owned by the Canons of Bolton Abbey in North Yorkshire who, towards the end of the 12th century, let the estate to a family who took the surname 'Wentworth'. It was they who built the first Wentworth Woodhouse which may well have been constructed of wood but the name signifies 'the house in the wood'. When it was sold following the death of the 8th Earl, part of the house became an Education College for a time. It is now a private residence.

Leave the track here and bear slightly right across the park, walk alongside a rustic fence to rejoin the drive which leads past the elegant stable block designed by John Carr before reaching the road. Cross into Clayfield Lane, passing the Round House which once served as a windmill for the estate, but 50 yards beyond the cricket pavilion, go left through a gate, across a grassy play area and back to the car park.

• The Round House, Wentworth.

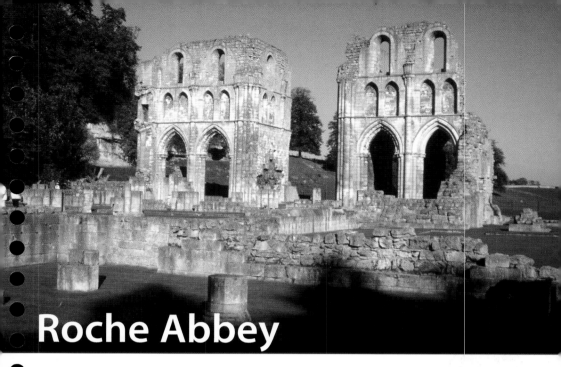

Roche Abbey

Laughton en le Morthen - St. John's - Firbeck - Roche Abbey - Slade Hills

Introduction

A very pleasant walk through attractive rolling countryside on the eastern margins of South Yorkshire. It encounters open fields, woodland glades, gentle hills, quiet villages, sleepy hamlets and the evocative ruins of a Cistercian Abbey. All of the paths and tracks are well defined but sections can be rather muddy after wet weather.

Points of interest

The village of Laughton with its splendidly ornate church and red pantile roofs; Firbeck and St. Martin's Church; the impressive ruins of Roche Abbey, founded in 1147 by Richard de Busli and Richard Fitz Turgis; the Slade Hills from where there are extensive views over the South Yorkshire countryside.

Information

Distance & time:	7.5 miles (12km). 3–4hrs. not including stops.
Start & finish:	All Saints Church, Laughton en le Morthen. (Grid Ref: 517882)
Map:	OS Explorer 279 Doncaster
Parking:	limited parking near All Saints Church. Roadside parking in Laughton.
Public Transport:	daily bus services from Rotherham. Service No. 19. Tel: South Yorks. Passenger Transport (01709) 515151.
Refreshments:	Pubs in Laughton & Firbeck
Tourist Information:	Central Library, Walker Place, Rotherham. S65 1JH. Tel: 01709 823611.
Roche Abbey:	For opening times and further information contact: Roche Abbey Tel: (0114) 276 8688

• A re-enactment in the grounds of Roche Abbey

Directions

1. Walk to the far end of Church Corner, passing All Saints Church on the right, to climb a stile into a field. Bear left alongside a wall, crossing another stile into a very humocky field. Continue ahead following the line of a hawthorn hedge on the right which leads to a stile in the far corner. Climb the stile onto a narrow, hedged in path, passing school playing fields before descending steps onto the road. Cross to a kissing gate with footpath sign and continue ahead, following the line of a hedge on the left after 40 yds. The path runs across the top of a field, then crosses a field before passing to the left of St. John's Church and the road.

Unfortunately, the church of St John the Baptist, Throapham, is now pastorally redundant and is now in the care of The Churches Conservation Trust.

2. Cross the road, bearing left on the far side for 50 yds. to a Public Bridleway sign pointing to the right. Follow the direction of the sign through open fields, keeping left of a fied ditch before going left to cross a plank footbridge over a stream, then on through more fields. After a gentle rise the path becomes hedged in for a short distance, then fenced in as it descends towards the left-hand end of Thorn Thwaite Wood which is passed on the left

On warm summer days the pungent smell of wild garlic fills the air along this stretch of the walk, whilst in spring the floor of the wood is carpeted with bluebells.

At the end of the wood the path continues along a hedged in green lane, with an abundance of wild flowers on either side and birds chirping and singing from the overhanging boughs. At the end of the green lane bear right, then left around a house to follow a track down to a country lane known as Penny Hill. Continue straight ahead, over Thwaite House Bridge and along the gently rising lane to a junction with a road. Go right along the road into the village of Firbeck.

3. On reaching St Martin's Church go left on a footpath alongside the churchyard into a field. Continue straight ahead onto a broad field track which swings first left, then slightly right to join another track at a 'T' junction. Turn right here, continuing along the track and round a sharp left-hand bend to a Public Bridleway sign pointing to the right across a field. Leave the track to follow the bridleway which descends to the right of a house, passes through a gateway then continues along a dirt track into the pretty hamlet of Stone. The track swings right on entering the hamlet, past the clematis clad buildings of Stone Mill and over Firbeck Dyke to a junction with a narrow lane. Go left here up the gently rising lane to pass through a gate with a footpath sign on the left.

4. Bear right across the field on an indistinct footpath which heads towards a stile in front of a house. Once over the stile turn right up a lane to a junction with the busy Maltby - Blyth Road which is followed to the left for 40yds. to a footpath sign by the side of a white gate. Climb the well worn stile over the wall then bear right along the field, heading towards Roche Abbey which lies directly ahead. To explore the Abbey grounds and ruins, continue along the path skirting the left-hand boundary fence of the Abbey to Abbey House where admission can be gained.

5. To continue the walk retrace your steps along the footpath to the corner of the Abbey grounds. Turn right here alongside the boundary fence to cross a stile then the Abbey brook. Shortly after passing a waterfall tumbling from Laughton Pond on the right, keep to the left-hand path through King's Wood to a 'Y' fork and yellow waymarker. Take the left fork which climbs to a stile on the right at the top of the rise. Cross the stile, bearing right around the edge of the field on a footpath which runs along the crest of the Slade Hills.

6. Occasional gaps through the trees on the right give glimpses of the surrounding countryside and a couple of strategically placed benches offer the chance to rest the legs and take in the fine scenery. The field edge path eventually descends from the escarpment to join a track at a point where power lines pass overhead. At a footpath sign go right, off the main track onto a subsidiary track, heading towards the ornate spire of Laughton church. The track peters out in a field but continue ahead to a gap in the hedge on the left with a yellow waymarker. Pass through the gap, bearing right on the opposite side for 20 yds. to pass through another gap in the hedge, this time on the right. Once through this go left, alongside the hedge, on a field path which descends to climb an iron stile into a narrow, often boggy, field. Cross to a simmilar stile on the far side, then bear left up the the next field to the St Ledger Inn. On reaching the road turn right through the village to return to All Saints Church.

High & Low Bradfield
Sheffield's little lake district

**Low Bradfield - Dale Dike Reservoir - Strines Reservoir - Hallfield -
Agden Reservoir - High Bradfield**

Introduction

The Bradfield Valley, just seven miles north-west of Sheffield, is a secluded spot that appears to have been side-stepped by the hustle and bustle of the city. Sparkling reservoirs, splashing waterfalls, chattering streams, secretive woods, expansive moorland and quiet villages set the scene for this lovely walk through the area known as 'Sheffield's Lake District'.

Points of interest

The parish of Bradfield is the largest in England, covering an area of 54.5 square miles and with a population of almost 15,000, while Dale Dike Reservoir, which lies within its boundaries, was the cause of the most catastrophic man-made water disaster in Britain. Bradford Dale, besides its four glittering reservoirs, contains a mixture of open pasture, heather clad moorland, broad leafed and coniferous woodland, creating a diverse habitat for wildlife.

Information

Distance & time:	7 miles (11.25km) 3.5 hours approximately.
Start & finish:	Low Bradfield.
Maps:	OS Outdoor Leisure 1. The Peak District Dark Peak area.
Parking:	Free car park near Low Bradfield Cricket Ground. Grid Ref: 263919.
Public Transport:	Buses 61 & 62 from Sheffield & Hillsborough. Tel: 01709 515151.
Refreshments:	Pubs in Low & High Bradfield.
Tourist Information:	1 Tudor Square, Sheffield. S1 2LA. Tel: 0114 221 1900

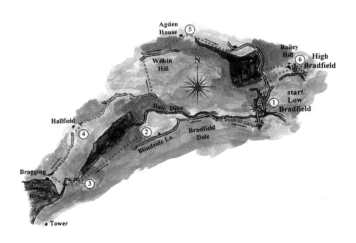

• The Cricket Ground, Low Bradfield.

• Strines Reservoir

Directions

1. The parish of Bradfield is the largest in England, covering an area of 35,000acres (54.5 square miles). The population encompassed within its 42 mile long boundary is relatively low however, at almost 15,000, due to the rural nature of the area.

From the car park in Low Bradfield go left along Fair House Lane, continuing along Mill Lee Road until just beyond the Plough Inn, where a broad track runs off to the right. Climb a stile beside a gate at the end of the track, follow a grassy footpath through fields with Dale Dike splashing along to the right, to reach Blindside Lane and go left along this.

Bradford Dale contains a mixture of broad leafed woodland and near the reservoirs, conifers where red squirrels are a highlight. The woodlands are the summer home of many migrant birds which come to breed here. The valley is basically Y-shaped with the four reservoirs of Agden, Dale Dike, Damflask and Strines collecting the waters that drain from the gritstone moorlands that ring this deeply incised depression. These were all built at the height of the Industrial Revolution, when water was needed both for drinking by the burgeoning conurbation of Sheffield and to power a variety of mills, tilt hammers and metal workshops that had been built along the River Loxley.

2. After approximately one mile and just beyond the isolated house of Brooms, go right along a signposted track that leads down into the dark pines of Dale Dike Plantation. Climb a stile beside a gate and proceed along a raised track with the brooding waters of Dale Dike Reservoir visible to the right.

This was the cause of the largest man-made water disaster ever to have occurred in Britain. In 1864, while the newly constructed dam was still filling, the earth bank that

formed the retaining wall collapsed, releasing 700 million gallons of water that swept down the valley in a torrent of tragedy. This was the infamous Sheffield flood in which bridges were washed away, houses, mills and workshops destroyed and 244 people died. The dam was rebuilt in 1875 but with a capacity of 486 million gallons, 224 million less than the original reservoir.

Proceed through two meadows to enter Andrew Wood.

An ancient broadleaf wood, predominantly of sessile oak, some hazel, birch and alder. The wood is rich in wildlife, including nuthatches, wagtails, great and spotted woodpeckers, rabbits, hares, grey squirrels and badgers.

• Dale Dike reservoir

3. After the wood continue through grassy meadows to a squeeze stile, cross a footbridge over a stream and walk on to a stile beside a gate. Once over bear slightly right along a wall-side footpath to reach a step stile, join a narrow footpath on the opposite side that descends through woodland to reach a footbridge spanning the conduit draining from Agden Reservoir, held captive behind the impressive embankment ahead.

During the winter months, when the reservoir is full, the gritstone-lined overflow channel creates a wonderful cascade of splashing waterfalls that glitter and sparkle in the low seasonal sunshine. A perfect place to take a break.

Follow the footpath up through the pine trees and through a meadow, heading for the buildings at Brogging where a rough track runs rightwards towards Stubbing Farm.

Visible from here, on the opposite side of Strines Reservoir, is the tall tower of Boot's Folly, built at the request of Charles Boot in 1926-7 in order to keep his stonemasons employed through a lean period.

Beyond Stubbing Farm, continue in the same direction through fields towards the impressive building of Hallfield, a seventeenth century building that was once part of the Fitzwilliam Estates but now a fine private residence.

4. A permissive footpath skirts the valley side of the house before joining a rough track on the far side of the property. Immediately before the gate leading to Thompson House Farm, bear left through the middle of a trio of gates onto an enclosed footpath to reach Dale Road. Turn right along this for half a mile, to just beyond a right-hand bend,  where a bridleway ascends through sloping meadows to join Mortimer Road.

Go right keeping right at the first junction and along Windy Bank to a stile on the left, 100 yards beyond the buildings of Wilkin Hill Outdoor Pursuits Centre. A path descends through Windy Bank Wood, crosses Emlin Dike before passing the little building of Agden House, a former shooting lodge tucked away in the trees to the left.

• The church of St. Nicholas, High Bradfield.

5. Continue in the same direction, crossing Agden Dike and walking past Agden Bog Nature Reserve.

A sensitive sphagnum bog that has remained relatively undisturbed for thousands of years and which contains a great variety of interesting wildlife.

The path now runs along the shore of Agden Reservoir before joining Smallfield Lane, which is followed to the right to reach a footpath on the left, just before the end of the reservoir and signposted to Bailey Hill. This climbs steeply at first through woodland before flattening out to reach a squeeze stile on the right.

Ahead at this point is the large mound of Bailey Hill, now crowned by wind-bent trees, but by far the best British or Celtic burial mound in the area and later the site of a Norman motte and bailey castle.

Once through the stile follow the path towards the splendid church of St. Nicholas in High Bradfield, one of the finest in South Yorkshire.

6. This very fine building, unusually large and imposing for such a small village, has stood guard over the surrounding countryside since the 12th century, though the present building dates mainly from the fifteenth century. The church commands a fine position and several benches in the churchyard afford magnificent views down the dale - a tilted patchwork of pastures nestling beneath the frowning moors of the Peak District.

Walk through the churchyard and through the main gates.

To the left of which stands the attractive Watch House, built in 1745 so that families of the recently buried could watch over the grave to prevent the activities of those involved in the loathsome, yet lucrative, trade of body snatching.

The walk goes right here, through iron gates and along an enclosed footpath skirting the southern edge of the churchyard, but it is well worth exploring High Bradfield which contains several interesting buildings and an excellent pub, the Old Horns Inn.

Pass through an iron gate through the retaining wall of the churchyard, bear half left through a field gate and follow a field path down to Smallfield Lane. Cross to the continuation path, descending steps to cross the overflow stream from Agden Reservoir before turning left and returning to the car park in Low Bradfield.

• The Watch House.

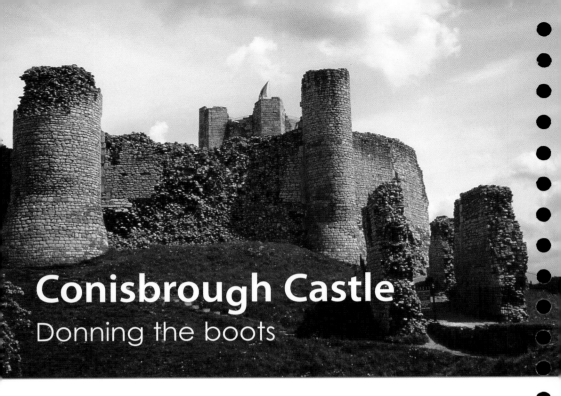

Conisbrough Castle
Donning the boots

Doncaster - River Don Navigation - Sprotbrough - Conisbrough Viaduct - Conisbrough

Introduction

An easy linear walk along the River Don Navigation from Doncaster to Conisbrough, with a chance to visit the splendid Conisbrough Castle, St Peter's church, the oldest building in South Yorkshire and the futuristic Earth Centre. Buses or trains from Conisbrough are used to reach the start.

Points of interest

Doncaster is a much improved town with good shopping facilities and a number of interesting buildings. The River Don is the principal waterway in South Yorkshire and has played an important part in its industrial development. Conisbrough Castle represents the most advanced late 12th century military thinking. St Peter's Church is the oldest surviving building in South Yorkshire.

Information

Distance & time:	7 miles (11.25 km) 3hrs, not including stops.
Start & finish:	Conisbrough Railway Station.
Maps:	OS Explorer 279 Doncaster & Conisbrough.
Parking:	Free parking at Conisbrough Railway Station.
Public Transport:	Regular trains from Sheffield to Conisbrough & Doncaster. Tel: 0345 484950. Bus service 288 & 290 from Conisbrough to Doncaster. Tel: 01709 515151.
Refreshments:	All types in Doncaster. Pubs at Sprotbrough and Conisbrough. Cafe at Conisbrough Castle.
Tourist Information:	Central Library, Waterdale, Doncaster. DN1 3JE. Tel: 01302 734309.
Conisbrough Castle:	English Heritage. Summer 10am-5pm daily. Winter 10am-4pm daily. Tel: 01709 863329.
Earth Centre:	Visits by appointment only. For opening times and further information contact: The Earth Centre Tel: 01709 512000.

• Conisbrough Castle

Directions

1. From Doncaster Railway Station, go left along Trafford Way, passing the North Bus Station to a traffic island with the splendid St. George's Church on the far side. Bear left along the A638 Barnsley/Wakefield road, first crossing the multiplicity of lines that radiate from Doncaster Station and marshalling yards, then the River Don Navigation. Immediately on the far side of the river go left and descend a flight of concrete steps, bear diagonally left at the bottom to join an enclosed footpath signposted to Newton. A rather fine, wooden arched footbridge is soon crossed over an arm of the Navigation before walking between the Don and the high, imposing walls of Crimpsall Prison. Another footbridge is then crossed and a footpath along the top of a raised flood embankment followed, with the river down to the left and good views of Cusworth Hall across fields to the right.

The rivers of Yorkshire have been an important means of transport since the earliest settlements and often determined the location and development of cities, towns and villages. However the Don, or Dun as it was originally known was a bit of a disaster as far as transport was concerned until an Act in 1726 permitted its partial canalisation and improvement along the valley towards Sheffield. Prior to this, boats relied on seasonal rains in the Pennines and high tides backing up the Ouse and along the Don and even then, Doncaster was the head of navigation. Once improved however, the river and associated canal network played an important part in the industrial development of South Yorkshire.

2. At Newton Lane Bridge Farm, keep left between the farm buildings and the river, pass

through a section of woodland just beyond here then join a footpath along the top of a flood embankment once more and walk round a large meander in the river. The path passes beneath a functional railway bridge, then a disused bridge, on the far side of which it joins a broad, well surfaced footpath.

This is part of the Trans Pennine Trail, a network of footpaths and rights of way stretching from Hull to Liverpool. It is Britain's first robust, multi-user long distance recreational route designed for horses, cyclists, walkers and as much as possible for wheelchair use

• St. George's Church, Doncaster.

3. The Trail passes beneath Don Bridge which carries the A1(M) high above the river before running alongside the massive electrified locks at Sprotbrough to reach Sprotbrough Bridge.

Prior to the building of the bridge, a ferry used to ply across the Don at this point, shuttling passengers between Sprotbrough and Wormsworth on the south side of the river. The little building on the north side of the bridge is the old Toll House but the payment of tolls ceased in 1888.

4. If refreshment is required at this point, proceed alongside the river for 150 yards to reach the Boat Inn. To continue the walk cross Sprotbrough Bridge, which gives good views of Sprotbrough Weir, follow the road round to the right but at a sharp left-hand bend, walk ahead along a broad track. Where the track swings left to pass beneath a railway bridge, proceed ahead over an earth bank to enter Farcliffe Flash woods.

5. This is a favourite haunt of cycle-cross enthusiasts and numerous trails have been carved out through the woods. The main track soon bears steadily left away from the river and ascends slightly between trees before descending to the banks of the Don once more in order to pass beneath a railway bridge. Stay as close to the river as is comfortable, pass beneath the multi-arched Conisbrough Viaduct and 150yds. beyond this, begin to swing left away from the river to eventually climb a flight of stone steps onto a broad track. Go right along this, passing to the rear of houses on the outskirts of Conisbrough, at a junction with a surfaced road continue ahead and begin to descend towards the town with Conisbrough Castle coming into view. At the bottom of the hill go left past the Castle Inn, turning immediately right at the end of the building over The Brook and along a footpath leading to Burcroft Hill road.

6. At the top of this go left along the A6025 for a short distance then cross with care into Conisbrough Castle Memorial Park. walk through this then ascend Castle Hill to reach the entrance to Conisbrough Castle

Conisbrough was made famous in Sir Walter Scott's novel - 'Ivanhoe' - where he wrongly interpreted the Norman architecture and building style as being Saxon. In fact even the earlier earthworks and timber defences were probably Norman too. At the time of its construction in the late 12th century, Conisbrough represented the most advanced military thinking of the time. At the heart of the castle is the recently restored keep, a massive structure made of magnesium limestone and the oldest circular keep in England.

The ruins that we see here today bear witness not to siege or the devastation of war, but to the tenuous fingers of decay brought about by neglect from the 1500's on. Under the rule of the Tudor Kings, nobles who graced the royal court no longer felt the need to fortify their homes and so diverted their wealth into the construction of comfortable

• Conisbrough from the castle keep.

• St. Peter's Church, Conisbrough.

stately homes. The age of castles was over, only the echoes of the past remain.

After visiting walk up Castle Street, keep left at 'Y' fork into High Street then turn right into St. Peter's Churchyard.

7. St. Peter's is South Yorkshire's oldest building and a place of worship for over 1250 years. It is thought to have replaced a former wooden church in about 750AD which in turn had replaced an earlier preaching cross. In Saxon times, St. Peter's was a Minster, or mother church, to several other churches in the area and much smaller than the extended church we see here today. Inside there is a wealth of interesting features including Saxon stonework, ornate carvings and fine stained glass including a 13th century window.

On the far side of the churchyard go right along Church Street for 50yds. then turn left into Wellgate, passing the ancient well on the right.

This was probably excavated round about 600AD, during the early development of Conisbrough and was used up to the early 1900's.

At the bottom of Wellgate cross a road onto a surfaced footpath alongside blue painted railings and follow this over the brow of a hill then down through trees to a junction with

Windsor Road. Turn right down this to reach the A6023 then go right again to return to Conisbrough Station where the futuristic Earth Centre can be visited by crossing the pedestrian bridges over the railway line and River Don.

• The keep, Conisbrough.

• The Memorial Gardens with the castle beyond, Conisbrough.

Lotherton Hall
Battles, beasts & brigantes

Lotherton Hall - Ringhay Wood - Hook Moor - Aderford - Hayton Wood - Cock Beck - The Rein

Introduction

A fairly long but easy walk through the lush, rolling farmland to the east of Leeds. There are many things to dwell on during the walk, including the village of Aberford; a place of great antiquity, The Rein, which is a 2000 year old earthwork built by the Brigantes to thwart Roman advances and Lotherton Hall, a small country house with fine family treasures, Edwardian gardens, magnificent bird garden and deer park.

Points of interest

Lotherton hall is the former home of the Gascoignes, the great land and colliery owners who gave the Hall, along with its grounds and fine art collections to Leeds City Council in 1968. Lotherton Hall Chapel is a fine example of an early medieval chapel. Lotherton Bird Garden is home to many rare and endangered species while in grounds can be found red and fallow deer and a herd of Highland cattle.

Information

Distance & time:	7.5 miles (12km) 3.5-4hrs. not including stops.
Start & finish:	Lotherton Hall car park.
Maps:	OS Explorer 289 Leeds.
Parking:	Lotherton Hall.
Public Transport:	Summer Service from Leeds Nos. 56/57 Sun & BH Mon only or Service 64/64A to Aberford. Tel: Metro 0113 245 7676
Refreshments:	cafe at Lotherton Hall. Inn & hotel in Aberford.
Tourist Information:	The Arcade, City Station, Leeds. LS1 1PL. Tel: 0113 242 5242
Lotherton Hall:	For opening times and further information contact: Lotherton Hall Tel: 0113 281 3259

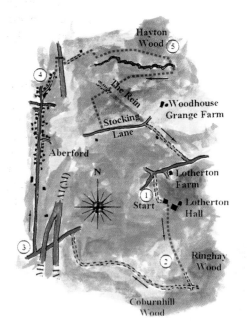

• Lotherton Hall

Directions

1. From the car park walk up through the Stable Yard where there is a cafe, gift shop, information point and toilet. At the far end of the yard turn right for a few yards then climb steps on the left leading to Lotherton Chapel and Hall.

The chapel is a fine example of an early medieval chapel-of-ease, built in the 12th century and unlike many other such structures dating from this time it never became a parish church. This is due to the fact that it stood in the parish of Sherburn in Elmet who's church served as the principal place of worship. It is also the reason why there are few historical references to the chapel, the earliest found being in a survey dated 1650. The entrance to the Hall is across the court yard from the chapel and is the former home of the Gascoignes, the great land and colliery owners. The house retains many family treasures including pictures, furniture, silver and porcelain along with a costume and oriental gallery.

Pass the lovely Edwardian Gardens on the left, created by Mrs. Gwendolen Gascoigne, continuing along a broad, flagged path overhung by trees and following the footpath sign for 'Boundary Trail and Coburnhill Wood' with glimpses to the right over the deer park which contains substantial herds of both fallow and red deer. Pass through a wooden gate into a long, narrow pasture where there are usually more hairy beasts in the adjacent field in the guise of Highland cattle, and walk through this to a gate at the bottom right-hand corner giving access to a fieldside footpath.

2. Walk down the left-hand side of the field, eventually walking alongside Ringhay Wood before a kissing gate leads onto a broad track through the trees. At a crossroads of tracks go right on a fine, grassy track that soon exits from the shade of the trees and contours round the edge of open, rolling fields as it heads towards Hook Moor and a junction with a shingle track which is followed to the right alongside a rustic fence with the embankment of the A1(M) just beyond. (Due to the building of the new M1/A1(M) link road, this section is different to the definitive map.) At a junction with the road go left, passing beneath two new motorway bridges before taking the first road on the right which leads into Aberford.

• Footbridge over Cock Beck, Aberford.

• An ancient scene of combat on the banks of Cock Beck!

3. A good footpath on the left-hand side of the road leads past the entrance to Parlington Park, then the superb Gothic style Almshouses built in 1844 by the sisters Elizabeth and Mary Isabella, noted benefactors of the Gascoigne family, before entering the village proper.

The church of St. Ricarius in the middle of the village dates mainly from the mid-1800's, but the site has been used as a place of worship for several hundred years. Ricarius is reputed to have been a chieftain, blessed with the gift of healing, who was converted to Christianity in the 7th century by Irish missionaries and who is thought to have passes this way during a missionary tour of this country in 630AD. A gruesome tail relates to a dispute between Aberford and neighbouring Micklefield which resulted in the death of John de Byngham, a local man slaughtered by armed men from Micklefield as he knelt in prayer at the high alter in 1247

Continue through the village, crossing Cock Beck, before bearing right alongside the Arabian Inn on a metalled lane with a small green to the left.

4. At the end of the lane continue on a footpath to the rear of houses which eventually joins a new footpath running left alongside a wooden fence bordering the motorway and up to a new footbridge spanning the broad carriageways of the A1(M). On the far side go right, turning left at the end of the rustic fence onto a track across the bottom of fields before crossing the drive to an isolated house and continuing along the left edge of a field. At a fence corner by a footpath sign go right, descending steadily to a gateway at the bottom of the field and once through turn left round the edge of a water meadow containing the meandering Cock Beck.

This little stream that flows for only 12 miles before emptying into the Wharf, has had two of the most fierce and bloody battles on record fought close to its banks. In 655 the combatants were Oswell, king of Northumbria and champion of Christianity, and the old pagan, Penda, king of Mercia. At the end of the battle, Penda, who for many years had been the cause of so much misery and bloodshed, lay with his generals and thousands of his army in a heap, the blood from their slain bodies turning the waters of the little brook crimson.

Just over 800 years later in 1461, it was the Lancastrians and Yorkists contesting each other

at the Battle of Towton, just two miles to the east. At the end, 38,000 of England's bravest and noblest lay dead or dying, their torn and bleeding bodies forming a human bridge across Cock Beck which the vanquished Lancastrian army used in order to escape from even more carnage.

• Lotherton Chapel

5. The path eventually skirts the southern fringes of Hayton Wood, but just before reaching the corner of the wood bear right across the pasture to a gateway through a hedge and continue for another 100yds before turning right to a pedestrian gate through a fence. This leads to stepping stones across the beck, some of which are not quite so stable as they appear so please take care, but once over bear right, climbing steadily through trees to a track running along the bottom of a sloping field. After 200yds. bear steadily left away from the track and up the field to a kissing gate in the top corner, then bear slightly left on the far side across a field (marker posts), heading towards a belt of trees that now cover The Rein.

This is one of several earthworks in the area believed to have been constructed by the Brigantes in an attempt to stem the northern advances of the Roman army. Today it is a quiet place with wild garlic and hearts tongue fern covering the floor of the earthwork and songbirds flitting through the canopy of leaves above.

Gothic style Almshouse in Aberford

Cross The Rein, continuing beneath overhead power lines on the far side for 200yds. to an electricity pole with yellow waymarkers nailed to it and turn left along a grassy strip between fields to a junction with Stocking Lane. Turn left along the lane to where it passes through The Rein, just before Woodhouse Grange Farm, then go right along a broad track running parallel to the old earthwork and up to a junction with a road. Go right along this back to Lotherton Hall.

• Flamingos in the grounds of Lotherton Hall Bird Garden

Kirkstall Abbey, Leeds
Ancient ruins & watery gems

Kirkstall Abbey - Kirkstall - Leeds & Liverpool Canal - Rodley - River Aire - Rawdon

Introduction

Only a few miles from the bustling centre of Leeds is a splendid wedge of green land through which the Leeds & Liverpool Canal and the River Aire cut a meandering course. This linear walk starts in Kirkstall Valley Park, in which stands the imposing ruins of Kirkstall Abbey, then follows the canal and river to Rawdon where frequent buses provide return transport.

Points of interest

Kirkstall Abbey was founded by the Cistercians in 1152 and is now one of the most complete of the major monastic ruins in Yorkshire. The Leeds & Liverpool Canal is a magnificent navigation that crosses the Pennines into Lancashire and is one of the most popular, but demanding, recreational waterways in England. Kirkstall Valley Park is a lovely green wedge of land well used by local residents.

Information

Distance & time:	6 miles (9.7km) 3 hrs. approx.
Start & finish:	Kirkstall Abbey, Leeds.
Maps:	OS Explorer 288 Bradford & Huddersfield.
Parking:	Abbey House Museum car park, Abbey Walk.
Public Transport:	Services 732, 733 & 736 Leeds - Otley, Ilkley and Keighley. Tel: 0113 2457676
Refreshments:	pubs in Kirkstall, Rodley and at Calverley Bridge.
Tourist Information:	The Arcade, City Station, Leeds. LS1 1PL. Tel: 0113 242 5242
Kirkstall Abbey:	Property of the City of Leeds. Open 9am - dusk.

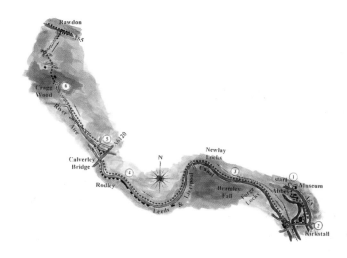

• The imposing ruins of Kirkstall Abbey.　　　• Water pours through the lock gates at Newlay.

Directions

1. From the car park opposite Abbey House Museum, cross Abbey Walk and descend past the Museum, which is unfortunately closed until next year, to a junction with the busy A65. Cross via the pedestrian lights to enter Kirkstall Valley Park with the imposing ruins of Kirkstall Abbey just to the left.

Kirkstall Valley Park opened in 1982 to protect and enhance the natural and industrial heritage of Leeds. It follows a green wedge based upon the River Aire, the Leeds & Liverpool canal and a series of footpaths and bridleways that link the areas main attractions. There are over 300 acres of gardens, lawns and recreational facilities in the park.

Bear left towards the Abbey where a gateway through the protective iron perimeter fence gives access to the ruins.

Kirkstall Abbey is quite unique in its location, positioned now in the busy northern suburbs of Leeds rather than in some tranquil and secluded setting, as in the case of most of Yorkshire's monastic ruins. In the past it has suffered greatly from vandalism but in recent years Leeds City Council have erected a protective fence, removed much graffiti and things have improved quite considerably. When the Abbey was founded over 700 years ago, this would have indeed been a secluded and tranquil spot with dense stands of woodland cloaking the surrounding hills and the crystal clear waters of the River Aire flowing serenely past; an ideal location for the austere way of life required by the Cistercian Order.

After exploring the ruins continue through the park in a southerly direction with the River Aire over to the right and the A65 to the left. At a fork in the track bear right, cross a bridge over a sluice system diverted off from the Aire then go left along a tree-lined path to a junction with Bridge Road in Kirkstall.

2. Cross with care then go right, crossing an ornate iron bridge spanning the River Aire followed by a railway line. Keep left at the traffic lights, cross Wyther Lane then walk across a small grassy area to a junction with the Leeds & Liverpool Canal. Turn right along the towpath beneath bridge No. 222 and past the old Kirkstall Brewery on the left which, unfortunately, no longer produces the amber nectar but at least the buildings have been put to good use as student accommodation. Continue past Kirkstall Lock which was painted by Turner in 1824 (I don't think they have been painted too many times since!) and on to Forge 3 rise Locks which raise or lower vessels a height of 23ft. 6ins.

Just beyond the locks and on the opposite side of the canal is Bramley Fall, a fine expanse of mature woodland that spills down from the suburbs of Bramley to the waters' edge and which provides pleasant walking for local residents on its many broad tracks and paths. Overgrown quarries here and a little further along at Newlay provided stone for sections of the canal, its bridges and also for much of Kirkstall Abbey many centuries before.

3. Proceed to Newlay Locks, another 3 rise flight which are one of the most attractive sets of locks on this section of the canal with trees and grassy areas on both sides creating a truly rural feel.

The Leeds & Liverpool is the longest single canal in Britain and without doubt one of the country's most dramatic and varied as it passes through some of northern England's most industrialised centres, through peaceful meadows and pastures then over the remote Pennine Hills on its journey between Yorkshire and Lancashire. The canal was started in 1770 with work beginning at both ends simultaneously, but it took 46 years before the two ends of this 127 mile long navigation could be joined by Robert Whitworth's 1,640 yard tunnel. Originally built as a trade route linking the North Sea, via the Aire & Calder navigation at Leeds, to the Irish Sea at the port of Liverpool. Little commercial traffic uses the canal today but it serves as a recreational waterway for thousands of pleasure craft and narrow boats

The canal is eventually forced round a large meander in the River Aire before running through Rodley.

4. The reason why the engineers decided to build the canal parallel to the river, rather than make the Aire itself navigable, probably lies in the fickle nature of the river. Following heavy rains in the Dales, the river's volume would increase dramatically, sweeping all before it and flooding vast areas of low-lying land. Conversely, in dry summers it becomes little more than a shallow stream, making it totally impractical as a reliable navigation

Rodley is a busy spot for canal traffic with a canalside Boat Centre, chandlery shop and plenty of mooring for narrow boats. The Rodley Barge Inn backs straight onto the canal and is a popular refreshment stop. Just beyond Calverley Bridge, which carries the A6120 Leeds Ring Road over the canal, leave the towpath by Owl Swing Bridge and turn right onto a cobbled lane between cottages. After 70 yds. bear left onto a paved footpath, descend steps then cross a track and bridge spanning the Aire.

• Moored boats alongside the L & L canal at Rodley.
• Horses graze in canalside meadows near Bramley.
• 6 miles down, only 121 to go! A milepost alongside the L & L Canal.

5. 5yds. beyond the bridge go left over a stile and through a grassy, riverside meadow where a stile at the far end leads onto a footpath beneath the railway line. Just beyond the bridge the path can become quite overgrown but shortly after crossing a small stream woodland is entered where the shady canopy of the trees suppresses the growth of many light-loving species. Just beyond the wood and at a bend in the river join an enclosed track then, at a junction with a surfaced lane, take the right-hand option which climbs steadily through Cragg Wood.

6. At a cross track continue ahead through a blue painted gate and onto a rough track then, at a right-hand bend by a footpath sign, bear left onto an indistinct grassy track that leads to a flight of steps and into a small field. Climb a stile on the far side, turn right along an enclosed footpath that can be overgrown at times, cross a lane to a stile on the opposite side then bear diagonally left through a meadow to a stile beside a field gate. Cross a lane then turn right onto a newly surfaced and enclosed footpath that rises steadily between fields before joining a lane past terraced houses in the outskirts of Rawdon. At a junction with the A65 turn right then cross with care to a bus stop on the opposite side for an easy return to Kirkstall.

• Rodley

Golden Acre Park

Five Lane Ends - Eccup - Breary Grange - Bramhope - Breary Marsh - Golden Acre Park

Introduction

Squeezed between the northern conurbations of Leeds and the River Wharfe is a tract of gently rolling countryside, criss-crossed by quiet lanes, trackways and footpaths, well known to discerning locals but frequently overlooked by many. This is fine walking country with the lovely Golden Acre Park right in its midst, and if you enjoy canine companionship, why not pop into the Leeds Dog Rescue Centre where there are always 80 dogs in need of a good walk and a spot of TLC.

Points of interest

Golden Acre Park is a lovely tract of land with expansive areas of grass, stately trees and flocks of ever hungry wildfowl on its lakes and streams. Breary Marsh Nature Reserve is an SSSI and a haven for a whole host of wildlife. Breary Grange is mentioned in the Domesday Book and despite only skirting its southern fringes, Bramhope is an attractive village and well worth exploring.

Information

Distance & time:	6 miles (9.7km) 3hrs. approximately.
Start & finish:	Five Lane Ends, Eccup.
Map:	OS Explorer 27 Lower Wharfedale & Washburn Valley.
Parking:	Roadside parking along Eccup Moor Rd. opposite Dog Rescue Centre. (Grid Ref: 283416)
Public Transport:	closest service is Nos. 34 & 35 Leeds - Alwoodley or 780, 784 & X84 Leeds - Bramhope alighting at Golden Acre Park. Tel: 0113 245 7676
Refreshments:	Cafe in Golden Acre Park. Inn in Eccup Lane.
Tourist Information:	Regional Travel Centre, The Arcade, City Station, Leeds. LS1 1PL. Tel: 0113 2425242
Leeds Dog Rescue Centre:	Eccup Moor Lane. Contact Amanda Sands. Tel: 0113 2613194

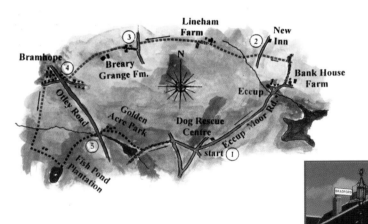

• Bramhope.

Directions

1. Walk along Eccup Moor Road passing the Leeds Dog Rescue Centre on the left and on towards the tiny hamlet of Eccup.

If you would like to take a dog(s) for a walk too, there are always 80 animals at the centre in need of exercise and the staff are only too pleased to oblige. Walking times are between 11am - 1pm at weekends, but from 11am - 4pm Tuesday to Friday.

The lane skirts the edge of Headingly Golf Course on the right with glimpses of Eccup Reservoir through the trees on the far side of the fairways. Immediately before Bank House Farm turn left off the road (bridleway sign) onto a rough track running alongside the farm and between fields to a stile on the left, 20yds. before the lane swings round to the right. Once over the stile walk along the left edge of a field, climbing a stone stile at the far side then proceed in the same direction across the centre of the next field to reach Eccup Lane. If in need of refreshment at this point the New Inn lies 100yds to the right and if you are walking a dog there is a lovely sunny, south facing beer garden.

2. Go left along the lane for 20yds. climbing a stile on the right by a footpath sign and walk along the right edge of a field, over a stile at the far side, then continue in the same direction (ignore a stile on the right) with a fence and small stream on the right and the buildings of Brockhouse farm over to the left. At the bottom right-hand corner of the field climb a stile beside a gate and walk along a rough track for 250yds. before veering rightwards off the track and across a large pasture towards Lineham Farm, just visible ahead. Climb a stile over the far field wall and cross the next field before passing to the left of Lineham Farm and onto the drive.

This is no longer a working farm but a residential centre for disadvantaged and disabled children. The contact with animals has not been broken however with several species of sheep grazing in the field just beyond the farm including a dark woolly Jacob and a smashing Wensleydale whose coat consists of a mass of dreadlocks. There is soon to be a donkey sanctuary on the site too.

Where the drive swings left, continue ahead over a stile beside a gate and along the

left side of two fields, then climb two stiles in quick succession before proceeding in the same direction along the right side of another field to reach a road.

• The carefully restored Lineham Farm

3. Go left along the road for 75yds. then turn right along a drive, past a dwelling on the right to climb a stile over a wall to the left of a gate and across the overgrown farmyard of East Breary Farm. Pass between derelict farm buildings which, at the time of writing have a planning application on them for conversion to private dwellings, to a gate leading

into a field and walk down the left-hand side of this but always bearing gently away from the field wall to reach a stile situated 20yds right of the field corner. There are lovely views from here along Wharfedale and into the Southern Dales. Once over the stile bear steadily away from the left field fence again to reach a stile over a wire fence, followed by a plank footbridge spanning a drainage ditch, then walk along the left-hand side of the next field with Breary Grange Farm on the left.

This appeared in the Domesday Book but as Brerhayh, a property belonging to Alward the Dane who also owned Eccup.

Climb a ladder stile then bear slightly left across the next large pasture, passing to the left of an isolated tree, to reach a wooden stile on the far side and continue in the same direction across the next pasture with a drainage channel on the right. Almost at the far end of this pasture the drainage channel is piped underground, bear right here to a stile in the field corner beside the white building standing on the Leeds-Otley Road and on the outskirts of Bramhope.

4. The pretty village of Bramhope has a history going back many years, but the oldest part of the present village dates from the early 1700's. The village has expanded

considerably from the small cluster of cottages that once surrounded the village square, the first big population increase taking place in the mid 1800's when workers and their families were brought in to construct the Bramhope Tunnel which carries the Leeds to Thirsk railway line beneath the village

Cross this busy road with great care then walk along the lane opposite, The Sycamores, for 250yds. where a stile on the left leads into a field and walk along the left-hand side of this and the next two fields, crossing Marsh Beck followed by a stile at the end of the third field.

• Walking the dogs, Eccup.
• The Square, Bramhope.

Walk along the left side of a wood, climbing a ladder stile over the first cross fence then go left along a rough field track, past derelict farm buildings on the left, to enter Fish Pond Plantation via a metal gate. Bear diagonally right through the trees to reach a three-fingered bridleway sign just below the retaining wall of the Fish Pond.

This is a quiet stretch of water with a small, wooded central island, very reminiscent of a mini Grasmere.

Turn left here alongside a small stream and through the trees to reach a rustic fence then go right over the stream via a footbridge, continuing along the path which runs close to the right edge of the wood initially before veering left onto the rustic walkway across Breary Marsh Nature Reserve.

This is one of the finest remaining examples of a wet valley alder wood in West Yorkshire. Alder trees and the Great Tussock Sedges which grow beneath them are characteristic of this special habitat which is home to a great variety of wildlife. Great Spotted Woodpeckers, Sparrow Hawks, Red Wings, Chiff-Chaff and Grey Herons are just a few of the bird species that live in the marsh.

At a junction with a surfaced track go right, beneath the busy A660 and into Golden Acre Park.

5. On the far side of the underpass a choice of route can be made. Either go left and follow the main tarmac path round to the right to the cafe and toilets and then on past the lake or, go right and along the right-hand side of the lake where there are better 'twitching' opportunities for wildfowl on and around the water.

Golden Acre Park was developed on the site of the old Black Hill Dam and opened in 1932. Some of its original attractions included a miniature railway, pitch-and-putt, rowing boats, a children's playground, paddling pool and a dance hall that boasted the

biggest dance floor in Yorkshire. Thousands of visitors flocked to the park initially but at the end of the 1938 season the complex closed. Leeds City Council eventually bought the site and the lovely landscaped gardens and shady woodland that we see today was started.

Continue beyond the lake to a junction with a broad, tree-lined track and go left along this to reach the road. Cross straight over and walk along the lane opposite, passing the entrance to Clonmore Farm on the left and back to the complex junction at Five Lane Ends.

• Feeding the wildfowl in Golden Acre Park.

Spofforth, Sicklinghall & Kirkby Overblow

Spofforth - Spofforth Hall - Stockeld Park - Sicklinghall - Kirkby Overblow - Spofforth Park

Introduction

A splendid walk through the rich agricultural land that spans the borders between North and West Yorkshire. The ruined manor house of Spofforth Castle is the starting point then field tracks, footpaths and quiet lanes link with the lovely villages of Sicklinghall and Kirkby Overblow before returning to Spofforth.

Points of interest

Spofforth Castle stands on the site of a Norman Manor House, built by the good friend of William the Conqueror, William de Percy. It was finally destroyed by Royalist troops during the Civil War. The villages of Spofforth, Sicklinghall and Kirkby Overblow are all very attractive, the latter being used for a number of film sets and TV programmes.

Information

Distance & time:	7.75 miles (12.5km) 4hrs approx.
Start & finish:	Spofforth Castle.
Map:	OS Explorer 289 Leeds.
Parking:	roadside parking near to the castle in Spofforth.
Public Transport:	Harrogate & District Buses Services 78, 78A, 78B & 79 Harrogate - Wetherby. Tel: 01423 566061
Refreshments:	Pubs in Spofforth, Sicklinghall & Kirkby Overblow.
Tourist Information:	Council Offices, 24 Westgate, Wetherby. LS22 4NL. Tel: 01937 582706
Spofforth Castle:	English Heritage. Admission free.

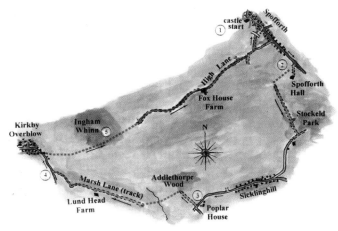

• Horse riders out near Sicklinghall.

Directions

1. In 1067 William de Percy came to England from Normandy and was rewarded for his loyalty by William the Conqueror who granted him 86 lordships in Yorkshire, including Spofforth. He established his headquarters here and built a manor house, nothing of which remains today. The oldest part of the present building dates from 13th century but most of it is from the 14th and 15th centuries. In 1309 Henry de Percy acquired the Manor of Alnwick in Northumberland and as the family gained more power and influence in the north-east, the importance of Spofforth declined and records show that it was last occupied around 1604.

The castle began to fall into decay, bits were purloined for the construction of other dwellings in Spofforth and the place was finally reduced to a shell by Cromwell during the Civil War.

Walk through the village heading towards Wetherby, passing first the Castle Inn on the right, then the Railway Inn on the left, the latter being a reminder of the days when the village was served by a rail connection between Harrogate and Wetherby. Keep to the footpath on the right-hand side of the road which leads out of the village before joining the drive to Spofforth Hall. Go right along this for a short distance but where it swings left towards the Hall, continue ahead onto a rough field track and along the left-hand side of a field.

Spofforth Hall has changed hands many times during this century. Originally constructed as a family home, it was occupied by the Army during the Second World War. Following this it served as a shelter for depressed mothers and neglected children before reverting to its present function as a Cheshire Home in the 1950's.

2. Continue on in this same direction, eventually joining a fenced in track for a while before walking alongside a rustic fence bounding Stockeld Park. At a 'T' junction with a broad track go right through woodland and past a nursery on the left, at which point the track becomes a surfaced lane that leads into the eastern end of the village of Sicklinghall. Bear right through this attractive village of charming cottages, robust houses and well tended gardens, passing first the duck pond then the Catholic Church of Mary Immaculate before reaching the Scotts Arms on the right.

This and many other buildings had to be rebuilt following a devastating fire that swept through the village in 1685. Following this, it became a popular refreshment stop for wealthy families out for a carriage ride from Harrogate, Wetherby and Harewood. Today it serves fine ales and mouthwatering meals and is extremely popular.

Proceed through the village, passing the daffodil adorned village sign and on along Kirkby Lane.

3. Just beyond the red brick buildings of Poplar House and immediately before a junction with Paddock House Lane, both on the left, go right along a broad, unsurfaced track. After 350yds. and just before a white gate turn left off the track onto a footpath skirting to the left of Addlethorpe Wood. The path swings gently rightwards and descends to  negotiate a kissing gate and stream before crossing open pasture. At one point the path runs close to the right-hand field fence, passes beneath the boughs of an overhanging tree, then bears away from the fence again before reaching a kissing gate on the far side of the pasture. This gives access to Marsh Lane, an ancient track that once linked Wetherby to Skipton.

It is rather narrow in places and can be very muddy, especially after rain and when horses have churned up the ground. Stay on this track, passing the buildings of Lund Head Farm on the left, before the track swings right and joins Barrowby Lane on the outskirts of Kirkby Overblow.

4. Turn right and walk towards the village with splendid views over the Southern Dales and Almscliffe Crag to the left.

Kirkby Overblow is a real gem of a village that probably developed around a place of pagan worship. St. Helen's Well in Swindon Lane may well date from these times and the lovely church of All Saints, with its fine 15th century tower, stands on a site that has been used for Christian worship for over 1,000 years. The name 'Overblow' is derived from activities that took place in the area during the Middle Ages. The area is rich in iron ore

and forges were manned by people called 'ore blowers'. The village has attracted the attentions of a number of film and TV directors in the past and has starred in both 'Langley Bottom' and 'Parkin's Patch'.

• Spofforth Castle from Castle Green.
• Sicklinghall.

To explore this attractive village or make use of one of its hostelries carry on along the lane, but to continue the walk, turn right at a small grassy island crowned with two large trees just beyond the first row of houses on the right, onto a track and across a cattle grid before entering a field. Pass through the pedestrian gate to the right of the cattle grid then

bear right round the edge of the field with houses to the right. Pass through a gate at the end of the field and continue round the right edge of the next field to reach another gate on the right.

Once through go left, over a stile through a wall and across a section of open pasture before walking alongside a wall and on through two more fields. Cross a stile over the wall just before the end of the second field, turning right on the far side to a pedestrian gate leading into Ingham Whinn, an enclosed section of woodland rich in birdlife and carpeted with bluebells in spring.

5. Walk along the right edge of the wood, exiting at another pedestrian gate on the far side, then join a rough track along the right edge of fields. The track eventually improves, passes the buildings of Fox Heads Farm on the right, before it becomes surfaced and known as High Lane. 20yds. after crossing Toad Hole Beck and just before the lane begins to rise towards houses in Spofforth, go left through a gate and along a raised track through a field.

After passing beneath the old railway bridge keep left alongside a wall, through the car park of the Castle Inn and on to the road in Spofforth. Turn left back to the castle.

• Stormy skies over Spofforth.
• Poppies add a splash of colour to the hedgerows in Stockeld Park

Holmfirth

Holmfirth - Ramsden Reservoir - Holme - Digley Reservoir - Upper Stubbins

Introduction

Star of canvas, film and novel, this part of Pennine Yorkshire is one of the best known landscapes in the world and rightly so. Holmfirth, the starting point of the walk, is revered for being the setting of the television classic, 'Last of the Summer Wine', but the real atmosphere of the place is best experienced on the open, windswept moors above the town.

Points of interest

Holmfirth is the epitome of a Victorian mill town with its double-decker, gritstone cottages rising steeply up the sides of the Pennine Hills. Sid's Café and other places in Holmfirth are well visited by the folk in search of nostalgic film locations, as is Ashley Jackson's Gallery in Huddersfield Road, where the atmosphere of the surrounding hills can be experienced even on the most miserable of days. The reservoirs of the Upper Holme Valley are lovely stretches of water and a haven for wildlife, yet they have been the cause of disasters in the past.

Information

Distance & time:	8.5 miles (13.7km). 4 - 4.5 hours, not including stops.
Start & finish:	Holmfirth Tourist Information Office.
Maps:	OS Outdoor Leisure 1 The Peak District Dark Peak Area or OS Explorer 288 Bradford & Huddersfield.
Parking:	Several car parks in Holmfirth.
Public Transport:	Buses from Barnsley, Huddersfield, Marsden, Penistone, Wakefield & Sheffield.
Refreshments:	All types in Holmfirth. Pub at Holme.
Tourist Information:	49/51 Huddersfield Road, Holmfirth. HD7 1JP. Tel: 01484222444.

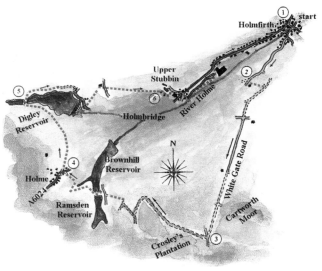

• A view over Holmfirth from Holme Lane.

Directions

1. From the Tourist Office, cross Huddersfield Road and enter Victoria Street, turning right shortly after crossing the River Holme into Rotcher Road, which climbs steeply past solid looking gritstone houses and terraced cottages.

Holmfirth is a splendid example of a Victorian mill town, with its buildings made and roofed of local gritstone and rising steeply up the hillsides above the Holme Valley. Due to the restricted space in the valley, many of the houses are split level, or 'double-deckers' as they are known locally, with four storeys split into two sets of two. Many of the cottages still retain weaver's windows in the upper storey from the time when hand-looms were installed in many of the houses prior to the advent of powered looms. The windows reach from floor level to the eaves of the roof, so maximising the light entering the weaving room.

Turn right into Cemetery Road, follow this away from the town for approximately a quarter of a mile, with ever improving views along the Holme Valley.

2. Turn left along a grassy track opposite a recently restored farm cottage and climb to derelict farm buildings. Pass between the buildings to join a broad track and turn right along this, now with magnificent views back over Holmfirth, across the surrounding moors and towards the Jubilee Tower, prominent on Castle Hill above Huddersfield. Proceed ahead over a cross-roads, now on a surfaced road known as White Gate Road that runs along the crest of Cartworth Moor.

There are many outstanding views from this high vantage point, with the Peak District Moors to the left and the expanses of the Pennines to the right. Just beyond the isolated Moorfield Farm the tarmac ends and the way continues along a broad, un-surfaced track that runs straight as a dye into the remote beauty of the hills.

Even in our milder winters snow often covers these moors and a crisp, white covering is not uncommon in late spring, when lambs are suddenly confronted with the harsh reality

of life here. Summer can be a joyous time however, with acres of purple heather stretching as far as the eye can see and the air filled with the chirpy song of the skylark and the evocative fluting call of the curlew.

• Holmfirth.

3. At a junction with a road, cross onto another track, known as Ramsden Road and follow this past Crossley's Plantation before swinging gently left round the northern edge of Ramsden Edge. At a track junction in front of a plantation turn right and descend steadily, but at a left-hand bend turn right off the main track onto a grassy footpath leading to a stile over a wall. Once over, go left along a track that descends through trees to reach the parking and picnic area above Ramsden Reservoir.

Turn right along the road for 100yds then bear sharp left onto the footpath that descends to cross the dam wall between Ramsden and Browhill Reservoirs. On the far side turn right along a footpath that contours around a quiet arm of Rake Dike and crosses a footbridge spanning a superb cascade that plunges into a deep, dark pool. Follow the obvious footpath that eventually climbs into the village of Holme.

4. This is a typical Pennine village with solid gritstone buildings nestling beneath the dark, peaty mass of Black Hill. The village developed around agriculture as can be seen from the number of barns that line the A6024 Woodhead Road that bisects the village. In the early 1800's many of the inhabitants supplemented their incomes by hand-loom weaving and some of their multi-windowed houses can still be seen today.

Turn left through the village but after 100yds go right through a cobbled square and onto a lane. However if refreshment is required, continue for a further 50yds to reach the Fleece Inn. After 80yds turn right through an iron gate beside a barn onto a track which forms part of the Kirklees Way. Climb a stile beside a gate, cross a field to reach a stile 40yds below its far top corner, then continue along the well marked footpath that contours round the edge of Stopes Moor and heads towards Digley Reservoir. At a junction with a well-engineered footpath go left and follow this over the dam wall that separates Bilberry and Digley Reservoirs.

Bilberry Dam was the cause of a terrible disaster during the winter of 1852. Heavy rains

during the first few days of February had filled the reservoir to capacity and in the early hours of the 5th, it burst, releasing a torrent of water that rushed down the narrow Holme Valley towards Holmfirth. Trees, mills, cottages, farms and animals were washed away and 81 people lost their lives.

• Clouds swirl around the Pennines near Dingley.
• The overflow sluice at Dingley Reservoir.

5. Follow the obvious track on the far side, turning right at a junction of tracks and walk along the northern edge of Digley Reservoir to pass a car park and picnic site.

This area is internationally important for bird conservation and Yorkshire Water has created new paths and recreational areas in order to minimise visitor impact on the landscape and its wildlife. Tufted Ducks and Little Grebes are common on the water while Pied Flycatcher and Green Woodpecker inhabit the woodland. The moorlands that encircle the reservoir are home to Curlew, Ring Ouzel and the rare Golden Plover.

Turn right through a gate opposite the car park, descend steps and follow the path that runs parallel with the road. At a junction with the road turn right for 400yds (don't cross the road over the dam wall) pass the overflow sluices of the reservoir on the right, then go left up steps to a kissing gate and ascend the left side of a field. Climb a stile over a wall to the rear of houses at Bank Top, walk along the right edge of a field to a kissing gate, then bear diagonally left across the next field to reach a gateway leading onto a rough track. Turn right here, passing houses at Austonley, climb a stile over a wall on the left then go right to a junction with a lane. Cross straight over onto a track beside a house, climb a stile over a wall at its far end and turn right through several fields.

6. At a junction with an enclosed track, above the mill ponds of Upper Stubbin Mill, turn right, cross a lane then go left just before a white painted house onto a paved footpath leading into a field. At the far end turn left through a gate onto a walled track that

descends to cross the mill race. At a junction with Yew Tree Lane turn right, go right again into Fairfields Road before crossing the A6024 into Co-op Lane then after 50yds swing left along Water Street. At the end join a footpath that runs between the mill-race and Holme Water before skirting round the mill pond in front of Bottoms Mill and on to a junction with the A6024. Turn right along here and return to Holmfirth town centre, passing the Ashley Jackson Gallery on the left where you can once again drink in the atmosphere of this splendid Pennine hill country or even take a little bit of them home with you to hang on your wall.

• Snow dusted hills near Holme.
• The mill race above Stubbin Mill.

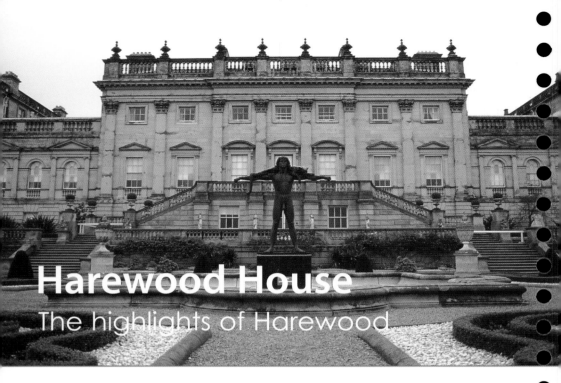

Harewood House
The highlights of Harewood

Hollin Hall - Harewood - Harewood House - River Wharfe - Harewood Park - Stank - Sugar Hills

Introduction

The soft, rolling countryside of central Wharfedale is splendid walking country, with a plethora of footpaths, bridleways and quiet lanes. This delightful walk takes in lush farmland, the village of Harewood, a lovely stretch of the River Wharfe, parkland landscaped by Capability Brown and above all, the majesty of Harewood House.

Points of interest

Harewood House is an elegant, honey coloured mansion surrounded by one of the finest parkland landscapes in the land. The attractive building of Hollin Hall was featured in the children's TV series 'Follyfoot'. The sparkling waters of the River Wharfe, backed by Almscliffe Crag and the rolling hills of West Yorkshire, create a gentle scene that has changed little over the years.

Information

Distance & time:	8 miles (13 km) 4 - 4.5hrs. not including stops.
Start & finish:	junction of Wike Lane & A61. (Grid Ref: 325431)
Maps:	OS Explorer 289 Leeds.
Parking:	lay-bye on south side of Wyke Lane. (see start)
Public Transport:	Metro service 36, 36A, 36C Leeds-Harrogate-Ripon. 781 & X35. Tel: 0113 288 6331
Refreshments:	Inn/Hotel in Harewood. Cafe/restaurant at Harewood House.
Tourist Information:	Royal Baths, Assembly Rooms, Crescent Rd; Harrogate. HG1 2RR. Tel: 01423 525666. The Arcade, City Station, Leeds. LS1 1PL. Tel: 01332 478301/2.
Harewood House:	For opening times and further information contact: Harewood House Tel: 0113 288 6331

• The Harewood Arms Hotel in the village of Harewood.

Directions

1. Walk away from the A61 along Wike Lane for a little over half a mile then go left through a gate onto a track at a public bridleway sign. The track makes up part of the Leeds Country Way (LCW) and is recognised by a yellow waymarker depicting an owl. A wise choice! Pass through a second gate then, 200yds beyond this, turn left onto another track with a signpost pointing to Harewood and follow the directions, veering left across a field in front of Spring Wood to a gate at the left-hand end of the trees. Pass through the gate then walk alongside Hollin Hall Ponds in the direction of Hollin Hall.

Some of you may recognise the impressive building of Hollin Hall, but not from your position in the fields of West Yorkshire but from your armchair, because the Hall featured in the late'60's children's TV series 'Follyfoot'.

2. Leave the main track a short distance before the Hall by bearing right across the field towards a gate immediately right of the garden wall, then pass to the right of the building and on across a field towards a pair of gates leading through a narrow belt of trees known as Cut Whin Wood. Ascend steadily up the next field towards New Laithe Farm, again passing to the right of the buildings before joining the farm drive which leads to a junction with the A659 Harewood - Collingham Road. Cross this busy road with great care, turning left on the opposite side where a good verge-side footpath develops just beyond the lay-bye and follow it for 500yds to a footpath sign beside a stile on the right. Cross the stile and walk along the left edge of a field, climbing a stile on the far side onto a track and go left along this.

3. The track becomes surfaced as it heads towards Harewood giving easy walking and a chance to enjoy the lovely scenery in this part of Wharfedale before emerging in Harewood village beside the Harewood Arms Hotel. To visit Harewood House cross the A61 and go left to the main entrance with the house some half a mile along the drive.

Harewood House, the home of the Earl and Countess of Harewood, is one of the most splendid houses in the country open to the public. The house began in 1759 when Edwin Lascelles, Whig Member of Parliament, asked John Carr to design him 'a palace' to be

paid for by fortunes made from Caribbean sugar. The beautiful honey coloured exterior houses a sumptuous interior of lavish plasterwork by Robert Adam. A marriage of two such talented designers could hardly provide anything else other than something very special indeed

• The weir beneath Harewood Bridge.

52

To continue the walk turn right along the A61 and right again on the outskirts of the village just before a sharp left-hand bend onto a rough track known as Fitts Lane.

4. On the opposite side of the road at this point and hidden by trees is the remains of Harewood Castle, constructed shortly after the Norman Conquests in order to guard a crossing point on the River Wharfe from marauding northerners. By 1209 Harewood had developed into a sizeable village based around the castle and local market. In 1657 the castle and its estate was sold to Sir John Cutler who reduced the ancient building to ruin for the sake of its timbers.

Follow the track downhill towards the Wharfe, turning left over a stile before the river and on along the edge of a riverside field. After 300yds bear right onto a track which leads into another riverside field and follow this towards Harewood Bridge but, when opposite the weir, go right down a bank and along a footpath leading to a stile and the road left of the bridge.

The River Wharfe is regarded by many as Yorkshires finest river. At this stage on its journey the Wharfe is a far more serene stretch of water than the youthful, fast flowing river of the Dales, but the weir beneath Harewood Bridge provides a fine sight and a spot highly favoured by anglers.

5. Cross the road to a stile on the opposite side, bearing left through the timber yard to pass to the right of 'The Office', then go immediately left to a stile and farm track. Turn left along the farm track for a few yards to a stile on the right beside a gate then walk around the edge of the farm garden and across a field to a stile on the far side. Once over this bear right past the rear of Mill Farm and on round the edge of the field where a stile in the far corner leads onto the Otley Road. Go right along this for 20yds. then cross onto a track (public bridleway sign to Stank) which rises steadily past Stable's House Stud Farm on the right to a junction of tracks. Continue almost directly ahead, crossing a cattlegrid on the brow of the hill, then descend towards the buildings of Harewood Yard and Home Farm, over Stank Beck and on along the Public Bridleway through Harewood Estate.

• Harewood House and the Terrace gardens.

• Harewood Church.

6. This wonderful parkland is largely the work of Lancelot 'Capability' Brown who was paid the princely sum of over £6,000 for the 9 years he spent at Harewood.

The bridleway continues towards a barn known as Carr House, then on through Stub House Plantation, bearing right at a junction with a track but 200yds from this veer left off the main track to a junction of tracks and go left again, following the LCW signs. The track eventually descends through Piper Wood before crossing an ornate bridge spanning Eccup Beck then on through parkland and several gates before reaching the A61 opposite Wike Lane.

• The Harewood launch 'Capability' cruises the lake.

Yorkshire Sculpture Park
A sculptured landscape

Bretton Country Park - River Dearne - Emley - Furnace Hill - Yorkshire Sculpture Park

Introduction

An unusual but most interesting walk through Bretton Country Park to the ancient village of Emley with its towering TV mast. The return leg passes ancient iron workings, created by Cistercian monks, before exploring the lovely landscaped grounds and free sculpture exhibitions in what was once a grand country estate.

Points of interest

Bretton Country Park was originally the deer park for Bretton Hall, now a college for the Arts and Education. Emley, famous for its massive TV mast, has a fine 14th. century church and an ancient market cross. The area was once rich in iron stone and formed a flourishing industry for Cistercian monks. Numerous outdoor sculptures can be seen in the free exhibition at the Yorkshire Sculpture Park, including many by Henry Moore.

Information

Distance & time:	8 miles (13km) 3 - 3.5hours, not including stops.
Start & finish:	Bretton Country Park car park. Grid Ref: 295125
Maps:	OS Explorer 288 Bradford & Huddersfield and OS Explorer 279 Sheffield & Barnsley.
Parking:	see start & finish.
Public Transport:	Service 441 Wakefield to YSP or 484 to Bretton Country Park. Tel: 0113 245 7676
Refreshments:	pub in Emley. Cafe in Yorkshire Sculpture Park.
Tourist Information:	Town Hall, Wood Street, Wakefield. WF1 2HQ. Tel: 01924 305000
Sculpture Park:	For opening times and further information contact: The Yorkshire Sculpture Park Tel: 01924 830302

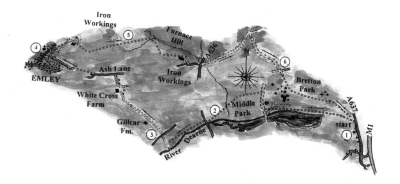

• An ornate bridge spans the outlet from Lower Lake

• Bretton Hall now houses a college for education and the arts.

Directions

1. Pass through the gate situated to the left of the Information Centre and enter Bretton Country Park, initially following a surfaced footpath followed by a short section of track before bearing left onto a grassy footpath that descends towards the ornamental lakes and past a Henry Moor bronze sculpture known as 'The Reclining Figure'.

Bretton Country Park was originally part of a landscape designed by Richard Woods in 1765, very much in the style of 'Capability' Brown. The two ornamental lakes were created by damming the River Dearne though the Lower Lake was completed much later than the Upper Lake. The Park covers over 100 acres and has the works of various sculptors scattered throughout, the most famous being Henry Moor who first visited in 1979 and expressed a strong interest in siting some of his works in this pleasing landscape

Continue past an ornate bridge spanning the overflow leat from the Lower Lake, cross a surfaced drive leading to a lakeside car park and walk past an enormous five part steel sculpture by Anthony Caro entitled 'Promenade'.

The land around the fringes of the lakes forms part of the Bretton Park Nature Reserve and is home to many species of wildfowl including a large flock of Canada Geese which tend to spill over into the Country Park. There is also a large Heronry in the Reserve.

2. At the far end of the field bear right to a gate through a rustic fence, turn right along a track and through an ornate iron gate then follow a broad footpath to a junction with a rough track. Go left (footpath sign to Clayton West), climb a stile beside a gate and walk along the right edge of a field with the massive Emley Moor transmitter mast dominating the skyline ahead and the misty outlines of the South Pennines beyond. At a fence corner continue ahead across an open section of field, climb a stile on the far side then bear diagonally left across a sloping pasture to a rustic footbridge spanning Bentley Brook and bear left again on the far side along a rough field track. Swing right at a fence corner, proceed to a stile beside a gate, once over bear left through trees to reach steps and a lane which is crossed into a broad, grassy pasture. Bear slightly left through this to a stile on the banks of the River Dearne, cross the corner of the adjacent field to a stile

beneath a tree, then walk through the next meadow but always moving steadily away from the right-hand hedge to a stile through the far hedge and a surfaced lane.

• Rhododendrons bloom in the grounds of Yorkshire Sculpture Park.

3. Go right to the Wakefield Road, cross with care to a gate and track on the opposite side (signposted Kirklees Way) and follow this through fields to buildings at White Cross. 20 yards before reaching the farm go right off the track, descend to cross a small stream then climb to a stile through a wall leading on to a track. Turn left along this, passing solid gritstone cottages and a barn, to reach Ash Lane and go left towards Emley. Immediately before the first house on the right go right to join a narrow footpath between fields, then continue along a residential road on the outskirts of Emley to alight in the village alongside The Green Dragon public house and opposite the parish church

Emley's most famous landmark is the modern TV mast and is visible for miles around, however it is not known how long a settlement has stood here, artefacts dating back to early Iron Age hunters have been found along with Roman coins but much of Emley's early history has probably been destroyed by extensive open-cast mining.

Today the village is a mixture of old and new with a number of modern housing developments surrounding the old village centre with its white painted market cross dating back in the mid 1200's. Legend has it that the 14th century church was to be built elsewhere in the village but during the night fairies moved the stones to the present site!

4. Turn right along Church Street but just beyond the Methodist Church go right along Thorncliffe Lane which soon becomes a stony track. Bear left at a junction with another track and follow this between buildings at Thorncliffe Grange Farm to a stile on the right immediately beyond the last barn on the right. Walk along the right edge of a field, continue part way round a second field where a stile through the hedge on the right leads awkwardly down into the adjacent field. Go left over a stile and along the top edge of a field then bear half right through the middle of the next field on an indistinct grassy track.

The undulations and silver grey exposures in this field are the spoil remains from ancient

iron workings. Following the Norman Conquests, some of the land in the manor of Emley was granted to the Cistercian monks of Byland Abbey, over 40 miles away near the North York Moors. These 'granges' were usually used as pasturing for sheep, but here at 'Bentley Grange' the monks developed an extensive iron stone mining and smelting industry using 'bell-pits', so named because of their shape.

5. Climb a stile in the far corner, walk along the right edge of another field then descend steadily through the middle of the next field with the wooded slopes of Furnace Hill directly ahead.

• The Paladian architecture of Bretton Hall

This is so named because the Cistercian monks built such a structure here to smelt their ore using timber from Bank Wood for charcoal and water in the beck to drive a water wheel.

Climb a stile, go right to a footbridge over a stream then bear right through the middle of a field. On the far side bear left on a broad grassy swathe alongside a tall hawthorn hedge, pass buildings at Bentley Grange before an iron gate beside a large gritstone block leads onto the farm drive which is followed to the road. Go left to a junction with the A636, cross to a grassy track on the opposite side which climbs steadily to a cross-roads of tracks on the brow of a hill and go right towards Bretton Park. Pass through iron gates and follow the obvious grassy path through the parkland setting to a gate beside the entrance to the Yorkshire Sculpture Park.

Founded in 1977, the Y.S.P. was Britain's first permanent venue for exhibitions of sculptures in the open air and now provides a unique setting for a number of works by Henry Moore. Born in 1898 in nearby Castleford, Moore often referred to the influence of the West Yorkshire landscape on his development as a young artist.

6. Numerous options are available here depending on your requirements and time available but to continue the walk, cross into the main drive leading to Bretton Hall, pass the entrance to Bothy Garden with its galleries, shops and cafe and descend to a track on the left opposite one of the halls of residence.

When Sir William Wentworth, owner of the Bretton estate, married a wealthy Northumbrian heiress in 1720, it gave him the financial freedom to build the Palladian style mansion that stands here today. In 1948 the Hall, lodges and lakes were sold to West Riding County Council who developed a Teacher Training College on the site. Bretton Hall College now has over 3,000 students studying the Arts and Education on what must be the most beautiful campus in Britain.

Go left along the track, over a cattle grid and through a belt of trees to re-enter Bretton Country Park where several Henry Moore sculptures lie close to, or a short distance off the main track which eventually rejoins the outward route close to the car park.

• An old barn at Bentley Grange stands on the site of ancient monastic iron workings.

• The parish church, Emley.

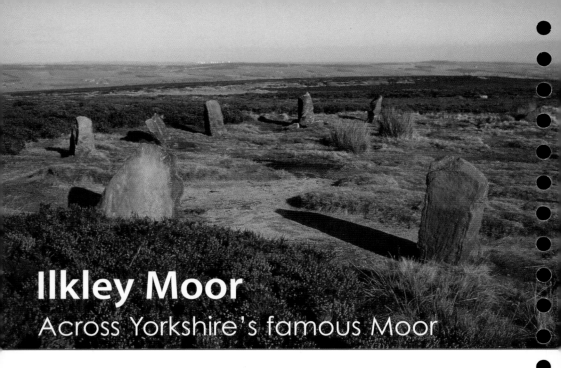

Ilkley Moor
Across Yorkshire's famous Moor

Ilkley - Cow & Calf Rocks - Twelve Apostles - Thimble Stones - Cowper's Cross - Keighley Road

Introduction

It is responsible for Yorkshire's unofficial national anthem, it is one of the most important Bronze Age 'art' sites in Europe and today, Ilkley Moor provides outdoor recreation for thousands of folk every year. This energetic walk from the charming town of Ilkley explores both ancient and modern aspects of this finest of English landscapes, however, sections are extremely exposed so be well prepared in case of bad weather and, I suggest you don't go 'baht' at'!

Points of interest

Ilkley is a charming and friendly little town with a good range of shops, cafes and pubs situated on broad, flower strewn streets. Cow and Calf rocks is one of the most famous landmarks in the county and a playground for rock climbers. Ilkley Moor is studded with archaeological phenomena such as the Twelve Apostles stone circle, numerous 'cup and ring' marked stones and the famous Swastika Stone.

Information

Distance & time:	6 miles (9.7km) 3 - 3.5 hours.
Start & finish:	Ilkley Railway Station.
Maps:	OS Explorer 27 Lower Wharfedale & Washburn Valley.
Parking:	several car parks in Ilkley.
Public Transport:	buses from Leeds, Bradford, Skipton & Keighley. Trains from Leeds & Bradford Tel: Metroline 0113 245 7676
Refreshments:	all varieties in Ilkley. Refreshment kiosk at Cow & Calf.
Tourist Information:	Station Road, Ilkley. LS29 8HA. Tel: 01943 602319

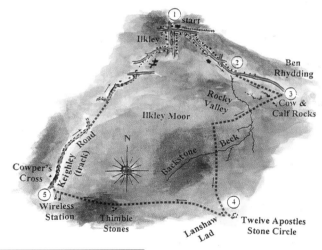

• Ilkley.

Directions

1. From the railway station cross to the Tourist Information Office and bear left, crossing Chantry Drive before bearing right up Cowpasture Road.

During Roman times a garrison was established here by the Emperor Agricola on land above the River Wharfe and known as Olicana, possibly on the site of an older settlement occupied by the war like Brigantes who bitterly opposed the Roman invasion into the North of England. It was largely a route centre and half-way staging point between Manchester and York. Although extensive development transformed the town during Victorian times, the lay-out of the fort can still be seen near All Saints Church.

In 1756, Ilkley's first bath house was opened by Squire Middleton at White Wells, heralding the town's emergence as a spa and with the upsurge in hydropathy in the late 18th. and early 19th centuries, Ilkley became a very popular place to be, with healing waters and bountiful fresh air from the surrounding moors. With the coming of the railway in the mid 1900's, Ilkley expanded rapidly with hotels, shops and fine houses being built for wealthy textile barons from Leeds and Bradford. Most of these solid gritstone buildings still line Ilkley's broad, flower lined streets, giving the town an air of Victorian and Edwardian gentility.

2. Where the road swings round to the left on the fringes of Ilkley Moor, pass through a pedestrian gate on the right and bear immediately left on the far side alongside a fence and climb a flight of steps from where a short, steep climb ensues through bracken, heather and bilberry. At a junction with a cross track go left along it, but just before it dips down to join the road, bear right towards the car park and refreshment kiosk below Cow & Calf Rocks. Bear right through the car park, past an information board and onto a paved footpath leading towards the most famous landmark on the Moor, Cow & Calf Rocks.

These are two huge rocks that dominate the skyline on this part of Ilkley Moor. According to legend, a 'Bull Rock' once made up a family trio but was broken up for building stone in the 1800's. These, along with other rocks and quarry faces in the area, provide good sport for rock climbers who can often be seen weaving intricate patterns up these exposed gritstone sediments.

3. Continue into the quarry where a number of fairly easy scrambles lead, with care, onto the rim of the moor or, if you are of a less adventurous nature, bear left in front of Cow & Calf and follow an easy path up onto the moor, bearing right along a broad path that skirts the now disused Hangingstones Quarry.

• Cow & Calf Rocks.

• The Twelve Apostles Stone Circle, Ilkley Moor.

• Cowper's Cross.

• The River Wharfe at Ilkley with Rombald's Moor beyond.

The quality of the gritstone on these moors has long been appreciated as thousands of tonnes of rock have been excavated over the years for buildings in Ilkley and along Wharfedale.

The path crosses the peat stained waters of Bakestone Beck then runs across the rim of Rocky Valley before swinging right above Ilkley Crags. At a cross track by a large pile of stones go left (south) across the flanks of Ilkley Moor, passing the odd cairn and striding the occasional stream before two sections of duck boards lead across areas of boggy ground. The path now rises slightly as it heads towards an isolated boundary stone, know as Lanshaw Lad, that marks the division between the Parishes of Burley and Ilkley and which is inscribed with several sets of initials and the year 1833.

4. The walk turns right at this point but it is well worth continuing along the main path for 100 yards to visit the stone circle known as the Twelve Apostles.

Information about these twelve squat stones is rather scarce but presumed to be of Bronze Age origin and, like so many stone circles with expansive views, a ritualistic meeting place probably linked to stellar or seasonal phenomena.

The continuation path is fairly narrow as it crosses White Crag Moss where the left branch at a 'Y' fork is taken towards a trig. point and cairn visible on the sky line that forms the watershed between Airedale and Wharfedale. A boggy section of footpath now leads towards a dry stone wall and a cluster of large gritstone boulders know as the Thimble Stones. Bear right along a wall side footpath across Rombald's Moor, sections of which have been slabbed with large gritstone pavers to reach the Wireless Station at Whitestone Gate.

It is easy to see why a transmitter station should be built on this lofty spot, with little to block the radio waves for tens of miles, but it looks rather incongruous on these barren moors where the only other signs of man's intervention are a few dry stone walls, the odd boundary stone or cross and the 'rock art' of ancient people. Cup & Ring marked stones are found all over these moors, carved out by people who lived here thousands of years ago in the late Stone Age and Bronze Age. The meaning behind them has been lost in the mists of time but these and the 4,000 year old Swastika Stone make Ilkley Moor one of the most important Bronze Age art sites in Europe.

5. Just beyond the Wireless Station bear right along a broad track known as Keighley Road with fabulous views across Wharfedale and into the Yorkshire Dales.

A short distance along the track and just off to the left is Cowper's Stone, thought to be the original base of a market cross transported here and a new 'cross' added some time later. This would hold true with the name because a 'Cowper' was a trader who may well have conducted his business from such a market cross in the Middle Ages.

Where the track swings round to the left continue ahead on a footpath above Spicey Gill to rejoin the now surfaced road by a tiny building. At a 'T' junction with another road, cross to steps and a footpath alongside Westwood Lodge that leads through trees beside Ilkley College. At a junction with Queen's Road turn right, passing St. Maregaret's Church, to a junction with Wells Promenade where a charming footpath through Promenade Gardens leads back into the centre of town.

• View across Ilkley and Wharfedale from Ilkley Moor.

Haworth & Top Withins
in the footsteps of the Brontës

Haworth - Brontë Parsonage Museum - Stanbury - Top Withins - Brontë Bridge - Penistone Hill

Introduction

Evocative Pennine moorland, peat stained streams, deserted farmsteads, crumbling walls, man-made reservoirs and a typical, gritstone hill village are just some of the ingredients of this classic walk that traces the footsteps of three talented young ladies. Add to this a stroll round the attractive old mill town of Haworth and a visit to the Brontë Parsonage Museum and a full days agenda is planned.

Points of interest

Haworth, once a disease ridden cotton weaving village, is now enjoying life as a major tourist attraction and its cobbled streets are lined with gift shops, tea-rooms and cosy inns. Brontë Parsonage Museum contains many personal possessions of the Brontë family. The ruins of Top Withins are reputed to have been the inspiration for Emily's 'Wuthering Heights' while Brontë Falls was a favourite destination for the sisters.

Information

Distance & time:	7.75 miles (12.5km) 4hrs. not including stops.
Start & finish:	Haworth Tourist Information Centre.
Map:	OS Outdoor Leisure 21 South Pennines.
Parking:	plenty in Haworth.
Public Transport:	Bus Services 663/4/5, 720 & 722 Bradford - Keighley. Tel: Metro on 0113 245 7676
Refreshments:	Pubs, cafes, hotels in Haworth. Pubs in Stanbury.
Tourist Information:	2-4 West Street, Haworth, West Yorkshire. Tel: 01535 42329
Brontë Parsonage Museum:	For opening times and further information contact: The Brontë Parsonage Museum Tel: 01535 642323

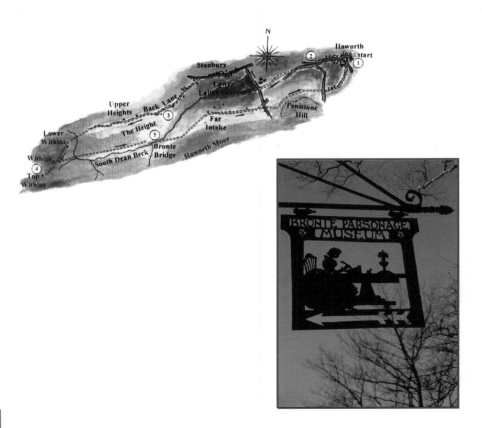

Directions

1. From the Tourist Information Office go right into the narrow, cobbled alley, signposted to the Brontë Parsonage Museum, passing first the Kings Arms then St. Michael's Church and the old churchyard.

The church contains the vault of the Brontë family, a monument recording the deaths of this gifted family and a stained glass window to the memory of Charlotte Brontë, while the churchyard contains the gravestones of the men and women who wrought this village; the builders and stonemasons, the spinners and weavers, the clog and bonnet makers; but one thing that strikes a sad note here is the number of children's graves. The attractive little town that we see here today is a far cry from the squalid, disease ridden hovel of the Victorian era, where typhoid was claiming the lives of half the children under six years of age and adult life expectancy was as low as 25 years, figures that could only be matched in the filthiest of London's slums.

Continue along the cobbled lane to the Brontë Parsonage Museum, home to the Brontë family from 1820 to 1861, and where Anne, Charlotte and Emily penned some of the greatest works of 19th century English literature. After visiting, continue along the lane, past the Museum's shop on the left, to join a footpath at the rear of houses before a squeeze stile leads into a sloping field which is crossed on a flagged footpath to its far right-hand corner.

2. At the road go left, keeping left at the 'Y' fork after 50yds. into Cemetery Road which has a grassy footpath along its right-hand verge. Just beyond the cemetery, bear right onto a broad, grassy track that descends steadily towards Lower Laithe Reservoir, passing the water treatment works on the right before a junction with Moor Side Lane. Turn right along the lane, past the end of the reservoir to a junction with Hob Lane and go left along this into the typical Pennine hill village of Stanbury.

This was the home of the last handloom weaver in Yorkshire, Timothy Feather, or 'Owd Timmy' as he was known. He pursued his craft until his death in 1910, aged 85, despite what must have been inexorable competition from the new steam powered mills. The

village evolved as a hill top settlement with good views in all directions yet close enough to valleys which provided the basic essentials for survival; water, fish, game, fuel and building materials. Many of the dwellings in the village have been, or are in the process of being, converted from what was obviously agricultural use.

• The main cobbled street, Haworth.

On the far side of the village bear left along Back Lane (public footpath sign to Top Withins, Brontë Waterfalls, Upper Heights) which is initially a surfaced lane between fields.

3. Shortly after passing Bully Trees Farm, the track rises more steeply, crosses a cattle-grid and then divides by a multi-fingered signpost. Take the right-hand track, signposted 'Top Withins', past the isolated farmsteads at Lower and Upper Heights and on into typical Pennine hill country, where the harsh cackle of the grouse, the occasional bleat from a sheep and the sigh of the wind, which always seems to blow across these vast, open expanses, are the only sounds you will hear. The sandy track becomes flagged as it runs along the edge of Stanbury Moor, past ruined cottages, barns and dry-stone walls before becoming a flagged footpath which ascends to the substantial ruin of Top Withins.

This ruined farmhouse is regarded by many Brontë experts as the one on which Emily based her much loved and world famous novel 'Wuthering Heights'. The ruins have received some remedial consolidation work in recent years in order to prevent further decay and stop lumps of the building being carted off by souvenir hunters!

This and the other ruins that lie scattered around these Pennine hills were probably constructed around the latter years of the 18th century in order to supply food to the increasing populations in the cotton spinning towns and villages. A bench just beyond the ruins is a perfect place to rest the limbs and enjoy a splendid panorama over these vast expanses of evocative Yorkshire moorland.

- Just one of the many signposts along the way.
- Top Withins, the setting for 'Wuthering Heights'.
- Brontë Bridge and Falls, a favourite with the sisters

4. After exploring the ruins and taking in the dramatic setting of this isolated old farm house, return along the path for 200yds. to Withins and down a steep path signposted 'Brontë Way'. Where the path forks continue in the same direction on the more distinct path to Brontë Falls, over stepping stones across a stream and on through rough moorland pastures above the peat-stained waters of South Dean Beck. At a fork in the path, just beyond a wall end, bear right and descend to a kissing gate which leads onto the footpath down to Brontë Bridge.

This quaint little clapper bridge is not the one that the sisters revered so much, but a replacement, constructed in 1990, to replace the original which was swept away in flash floods during the spring of 1989. It's easy to see why the girls enjoyed this idyllic hollow, being sheltered from the wind, warmed by the sun and lulled by the soporific sound of water tumbling over several mini-cascades.

5. On the far side of the bridge turn left on a narrow path that rises to eventually join a track running above a series of walled pastures and past the ruins of Far and Middle Intake. After crossing a cattle-grid just before a junction with a road, bear right onto a footpath signposted to Haworth and Penistone Hill, cross the road and continue in the same direction to a junction with a broad track on the edge of Penistone Hill Country Park. Turn left along this, continuing in the same direction where the track swings to the right, onto a footpath which skirts the edge of old quarry workings.

This was one of the main quarries from which stone was extracted to provide the street cobbles, roofing slates and building blocks for Haworth.

At a junction with a road cross straight over onto a walled track which descends past houses, turning left at the bottom along a flat, paved footpath that leads back to St. Michael's Church and Haworth.

• The remains of an old gate post stand defiant on Stanbury Moor.

• The tranquil waters of Lower Laithe Reservoir.

Heptonstall & Hardcastle Craggs
Mills, Hills, Deans & Dales

Newbridge - Crimsworth Dean - Shackleton Knoll - Walshaw - Hardcastle Craggs - Slack - Heptonstall

Introduction

Impressive scenery, historic interest and the lovely hilltop village of Heptonstall, with its two churches, make this a most memorable walk. It is a fairly long and energetic outing along clear tracks and well marked footpaths above Hebden Bridge, but the views from these exposed Pennine moors make it well worth while.

Points of interest

Heptonstall is a lovely hilltop village with many of its sturdy gritstone cottages dating from the heyday of handloom weaving. The churchyard is the last resting place of 'King' David Hartley, a local 'coiner' hanged for counterfeit. Hardcastle Craggs is an attractive beauty spot above the sparkling Hebden Water. Gibson Mill, one of the few cotton mills remaining in the area, is being renovated by the National Trust.

Information

Distance & time:	6.5 miles (10.5km) 3.5 hours only.
Start & finish:	New Bridge (Grid Ref: 989291).
Map:	OS Outdoor Leisure 21 South Pennines.
Parking:	Public car park at New Bridge.
Public Transport:	Buses and trains to Hebden Bridge from Halifax, Leeds and Huddersfield. Bus service H8 fromHebden Bridge to New Bridge. Tel: Metro 0113 245 76 76.
Refreshments:	pubs in Heptonstall, tea shop (at times) at Gibson Mill.
Tourist Information:	1 Bridge Gate, Hebden Bridge, West Yorkshire. HX7 8EX. Tel: 01422 843831.

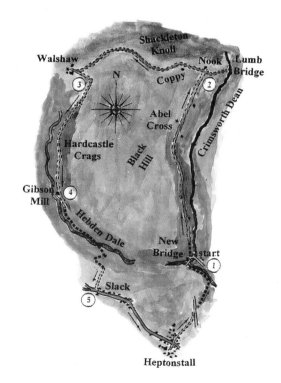

• National Trust cottages above Crimsworth Dean near the start of the walk.

Directions

1. 10 yards before the entrance to the National Trust car park, on the Hebden Bridge side of the road in New Bridge, follow the public Bridleway sign onto an enclosed track through woodland. At a junction with a tarmac track go right, climbing steadily up the side of Crimsworth Dean to just beyond National Trust owned cottages on the right where the track becomes unsurfaced. Continue on in the same direction, climbing steadily all the while to a pedestrian gate beside a cattle grid where the track leaves the confines of Abel Cote Wood and enters more open moorland.

The views now start to improve dramatically with beautifully subtle colour shifts from the deep greens of the pines in Crimsworth Dean to the pallid hues of the surrounding cultivated pastures; from the golden stalks of the moorland sedges that line the track to the dark heather that crowns the top of the moors

The track continues to rise past isolated farmsteads and the ancient Abel Cross, visible in a field over to the left near Charles Rough Farm, to eventually reach derelict farm buildings at Nook. From here it is possible to make a short detour to the right to visit Lumb Waterfall, an attractive spot for a picnic and quite spectacular following heavy rain.

2. Pass through a gate in front of the ruins, turn immediately left through another gate onto a broad, enclosed track that climbs steadily past more ruined buildings at Coppy.

The deep denes, poor soils and cool, wet summers in this part of the Pennines prohibited the growth of crops, making animal husbandry the only profitable method of farming. In good years they could chop down a few more trees and turn the land into pasture, in bad ones they may have been able to supplement their income with a bit of handloom weaving, but on these high, windswept moors, things must have been desperately hard. If you fell on hard times there was no welfare state to turn to and starvation was a common cause of death. The temptation to make money, by whatever means must have been great, and one local blacksmith did just that. David Hartley, along with his two brothers, Isaac and William, set up a counterfeit 'coining' industry from isolated farmsteads such as these.

Coining, or 'clipping', involved cutting the edges off legal gold coins, milling their edges

so that they still looked legitimate, then stamping out new coins from the smelted clippings. So profitable was this that Hartley became known in Calderdale as 'King David' and his brothers as the Dukes of York and Edinburgh!. The exciseman eventually got wind of the coining however and, despite the remoteness, Harley was caught and hanged at York in 1770. His body now resides in the churchyard at Heptonstal.

Proceed round the rim of Shackleton Knoll, the high point of the walk, which affords splendid views to the south over Heptonstall with the monument on Stoodley Pike visible on the horizon. Where the path begins to descend, go left through a gate in a wall beside a bridleway sign, turn right on the opposite side and follow a track which initially runs parallel to the wall but then swings left through the pasture. Pass through a gate in a wall, proceed past the lovely named Horodiddle Farm, but immediately after negotiating a gate leading into the hamlet of Walshaw, turn sharp left along a broad, enclosed track signposted to Hardcastle Craggs.

3. The 'tonstall' of Heptonstall, like the 'den' of Hebden and the 'worth' of Howarth, are all Anglo-Saxon names, but the 'Wal' here at Walshaw is of Celtic origin and means 'wood of the Welsh'. The native Celts, descendants of earlier Iron Age people, were largely driven westward by the Anglo-Saxons, but a few groups managed to persist in the remoter parts of the Pennine chain such as here on the wooded slopes of Hebden Dale. Today, Walshaw is a most attractive hamlet that has withstood the worst of Pennine weather for centuries.

At a fork in the track bear right and join the Permissive Footpath that descends through sheltered woodland into Hebden Dale.

This is quite a contrast from the stark exposure of the moor and a welcome relief on cold, wintry days when the wind cuts across the hills like a knife, penetrating every chink in ones clothing and freezing exposed flesh

The path runs past the beauty spot of Hardcastle Craggs, a series of large rocky outcrops on the right of the footpath that have been popular since Victorian times.

• Snow carpets the moors near Horodiddle Farm.
• Gibson Mill reflected in a snow fringed mill pond.
• The old, ruined church in Heptonstall

4. Eventually the path descends to Gibson Mill, a cotton mill built in 1800 by one Abraham Gibson.

The mill was originally powered by water stored in the mill dam, but this was unreliable during times of drought or when Hebden Water froze over in winter, so a steam engine was added in the 1860's. Due to competition from larger mills in Calderdale however, manufacturing ceased here at the end of the 1890's. The mill didn't actually close however, instead it took on a new role as a tourist attraction for people visiting Hardcastle Craggs. Various tearooms were developed along with a dance hall, roller skating rink and boating lake on the mill pond, but with the outbreak of World War II, activities stopped. The mill is now owned by the National Trust who are converting it into a Visitor Centre.

Just beyond the mill, bear right off the main track onto the lower footpath alongside the lovely Hebden Water. Pass two sets of stepping stones but at a third set, beside a Hardcastle Craggs National Trust sign, cross Hebden Water and bear left on the far side along a narrow, winding, uphill footpath that eventually climbs to the Scout Hostel. Just beyond the main building go right by a waymarker onto a stony track that rises quite steeply through Hebden Wood and at the top of the rise turn right along an enclosed track that leads into the hamlet of Slack. Turn left along the road and follow it all the way into Heptonstall.

5. Perched on the hills above Hebden Bridge, with dramatic views over the surrounding Pennine Hills, Heptonstall has a long history dating back to the Iron Age. Most of the buildings that stand here today however, were built during the 17th or early 18th century as weavers cottages and most have the typical 'weavers windows' just beneath the roof. At this time the bulk of weaving was done from home on hand looms as a cottage industry, prior to the development of large mills in the valley bottoms. The new church of St Thomas a Becket, constructed in 1854, stands beside the original church which was badly damaged by storms in 1847. It is possible that a church or chapel has stood on this site since the mid 13th century, but the first registered date is that of the old church in 1590. Close to the church is the old Grammar School, founded in 1643 and which now houses an interesting museum with lots of local artefacts, furniture etc.

Walk along Towngate, passing Weavers Square and the old Cloth Hall on the right, then turn left into Northgate where you will find Heptonstall Methodist Chapel, an interesting octagonal building dating from 1764 and which is reputed to be the oldest, continually used chapel in the world. Where the road ends, by a Calderdale Way sign, bear right along a rough track that descends steeply into Hebden Dale with fine views over Hebden Bridge and the surrounding moors. At a junction with a road, cross onto a footpath opposite that descends through woodland and over a surfaced lane before reaching Hebden Water. Turn left alongside this to the footbridge, cross onto a lane on the far side and walk past cottages in New Bridge back to the start.

A steamy walk in the
Worth Valley

Keighley & Worth Valley Railway - Keighley - Hainworth - Cliffe Hill - Haworth - Oxenhope

Introduction

A splendid day's outing in the Worth Valley with chances to visit the town of Haworth. made famous by the Bronte sisters. Keighley with its splendid retail facilities and revel in steamy nostalgia aboard the Keighley and Worth Valley Railway.

Points of interest

The Pennine town of Keighley has something for even one. with its modem Airedale Shopping Centre, welcoming cafes. individual shops and excellent leisure facilities. The Keighley and Worth Valley Railway runs for five miles along the Worth Valley from Oxenhope to Keighley and passes six beautifully restored stations along the way, Haworth, once a disease-ridden cotton weaving village, is now enjoying life as a major tourist attraction and its cobbled streets are lined with gift shops. tearooms and cosy inns. Bronte Parsonage Museum contains many personal possessions of the Bronte family.

Information

Distance & time:	5.5 miles (8.9km) 2.5 - 3 hours, not including stops.
Start & finish:	Oxenhope Station. (Can also be started from Keighley).
Maps:	OS Outdoor Leisure 21 South Pennines.
Parking:	free at Oxenhope Station.
Public Transport:	see KWVR information. Bus service 720 Keighley -Oxenhope.
Refreshments:	Pubs and cafes in Keighley and Haworth. Inn at Haworth Brow, cafe at Oxenhope Station.
Tourist Information:	2-4 West Street, Haworth, West Yorkshire. Tel; 01535 42329. The Town Hall, Bow Street. Keighley. Tel: 01535618014.
Brontë Parsonage Museum:	For opening times and further information contact: The Brontë Parsonage Museum Tel: 01535 642323
Keighley & Worth Valley Railway:	Steam trains every weekend throughout the year. Tel: 01535 645214. 24 hour info Line: 01535 647777.

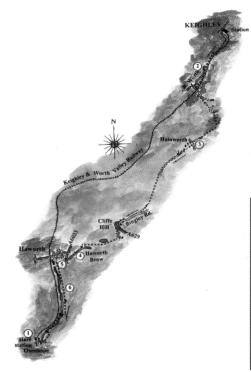

• Keighley Station.

Directions

1. Board the train at Oxenhope and enjoy the nostalgic days of steam as you ride the Keighley & Worth Valley Railway to Keighley. Alight at Keighley Station where the KWVR occupies Platforms 3 & 4 while Platform 1 & 2 offer mainline connections via Leeds, York, London and Skipton.

Platform 4 retains many original features including a cast iron canopy, waiting room, stone tower and cast iron water tank.

Walk out of the station, turn left along Bradford Road, then take the first turning on the left, a cobbled lane that passes alongside the station car park. Where the lane swings left beneath the railway bridge, keep ahead along a ginnel, pass through a tunnel beneath the line then turn right over a footbridge spanning a cutting before passing beneath the line again.

Cross a road and proceed along a track with the railway line to the left. After 75yds. bear left to walk along a wall-enclosed footpath which soon becomes a pleasant tree fringed stroll alongside the River Worth.

2. The riverside footpath eventually leads to steps and a junction with Woodhome Road. Go left along this, cross the railway line followed by Hainworth Wood Road and climb steadily to a junction with a track. Turn immediately right here along a footpath to the rear of houses before a fairly steep ascent leads to a kissing gate. Once through bear left to a stile through a wall, turn right along a partly surfaced track for 75yds. where a public footpath on the right leads through woodland. Pass through a gate on the far side, bear diagonally left across a field to a gap in a wall and walk along the top left edge of a field. Pass through a squeeze stile in a wall, walk along the right edge of the next field and proceed in me same direction to join a track and a junction with the road in Hainworth.

The area around Keighly, with its expansive hills and dales, vast open moorlands, quiet river valleys and solid gritstone villages, has been used as a backdrop to several films and TV programmes. 'A Touch of Frost', 'Moving Story', 'Treasure Hunt' have all had scenes shot in the area and the film 'Yanks', which launched Richard Gere's international film career, was partly filmed at Keighley Railway Station. Many documentaries about the Bronte family and their works have been filmed around Haworth and the Worth Valley, but probably most people's favourite is that endearing of films, 'The Railway Children', shot on location along the Keighley & Worth Valley Railway.

• The Keighley & Worth Valley Railway.

3. Cross straight over onto a lane past houses on the opposite side. The lane soon deteriorates into a rough track and then becomes a footpath that forms part of the Worth Way. At a junction with Bingley Road bear right into the village of Cliffe Hill and continue to a junction with the A629. Cross with care onto a track on the far side which swings first right, then left as it heads towards

buildings, but immediately alongside the first house go right over a stile and along the bottom of a field. The path eventually climbs the side of a bank above a small reservoir before swinging left and along the left side of the Three Sisters Inn car park at Haworth Brow. At a junction with Brow Top Road turn right with Haworth now directly ahead.

4. Immediately alongside the first house on the right, rum sharp right along an enclosed footpath, go left after 20yds. down another enclosed footpath between gardens and houses to reach the A6033. Cross with care into Dean Street and walk to the bottom of this, then go left along Prince Street to reach Brow Road. To visit Haworth continue to the end of this and turn left along Bridgehouse Lane which climbs into the village.

The attractive little town that we see here today is a far cry from the squalid, disease ridden hovels of the Victorian era, where typhoid was claiming me lives of half me children under six years of age and adult life expectancy was as low as 25 years, figures that could only be matched in the filthiest of London's slums. The town has been made famous by the works of the three Bronte sisters. Charlotte, Emily and Anne. If these three quiet girls could see Haworth today, they would no doubt recognise the steep, cobbled

main street and many of the shop fronts, but they would be astounded at the number of tourists who flock here from all over the world to gain a better insight into their past lives. St. Michael's Church, at the top of the village, contains the vault of the Bronte family, a monument recording the deaths of this gifted family and a stained glass window to the memory of Charlotte Bronte, while the churchyard contains the gravestones of the men and women who wrought this village; the builders and stonemasons, the spinners and weavers, the clog and bonnet makers: but one thing that strikes a sad note here is the number of children's graves.

• Keighley.
• Weavers Cottages, Haworth.

5. To continue the walk go left after 25yds. opposite Thomas Street, and along a footpath signposted to Oxenhope. Walk along the bottom of fields with Bridgehouse Beck and the line of the Keighley & Worth Valley Railway over to the right.

The KWVR as built in 1867 by local mill owners, but with train services 'franchised' to The Midland Railway which opened the Adjoining line to Skipton from Leeds and Bradford. The line became part of the London, Midland & Scottish Railway in 1924 and British Railways in 1948. It fell victim to the Beeching cuts of 1962, but a group of local Rail enthusiasts banded together and formed a railway preservation Society aimed at buying and reopening the line. In 1968 the society began running a regular service that has continued to this day. The KWVR is now what it has always been, a clean, well maintained smart and much loved private railway where you can enjoy the nostalgic days of steam aboard one of several steam locomotives. There is also the interesting Museum of Rail Travel at Ingrow West Station.

6. Cross a footbridge on the right, walk along a raised embankment, cross a track by a ruined house, then climb a step-stile over a wall and walk along the bottom of a field. Keep right in front of a house, but immediately beyond the gate leading into the yard, turn right and descend steeply to the beck and turn left alongside it. A metal footbridge eventually crosses the beck and once over go left on the opposite side along a surfaced drive and past the sewage works (nice pong!). Pass through a kissing gate on the right, walk along a partly surfaced footpath that leads to another bridge over the beck then go right on the far side. At a junction with a road bear right, cross the beck once more before arriving at Oxenhope Station.

• Fly Agaric mushrooms near Oxenhope.

Bramham Park

Bramham – Bowcliffe Hall – Bramham Park – Mangrill Lane – Bramham

Introduction

A gentle ramble from the historic village of Bramham through the rolling acres of Bramham Park, with a chance to visit Bramham Park House and its lovely French style gardens.

Points of interest

Bramham is a historic village, dating back to Roman times, with many Saxon, Norman and English Civil War connections. Bramham Park House is a splendid Queen Anne mansion, built in 1698 in the style of a Florentine villa and surrounded by glorious gardens that follow a formal French style. Wothersome is the site of a former medieval village.

Information

Distance & time:	6 miles (9.7 km) 2.5 - 3 hrs. for walk only.
Start & finish:	The Square, Bramham.
Maps:	OS Explorer 289 Leeds, Harrogate, Wetherby & Pontefract.
Parking:	roadside parking in Bramham village.
Public Transport:	bus services 770 & 771 Harrogate – Wetherby – Leeds; 175 Castleford & 780, 781 Knaresborough – Tadcaster – Wetherby. Tel: 0113 245 7676.
Refreshments:	pubs in Bramham.
Tourist Information:	Council Offices, 24 Westgate, Wetherby, West Yorkshire. LS22 4NL. Tel: 01937 582706.
Bramham Park:	open April – Sept (gardens only). Access to the house by parties of 10 or more only. Tel: 01937 846 000.

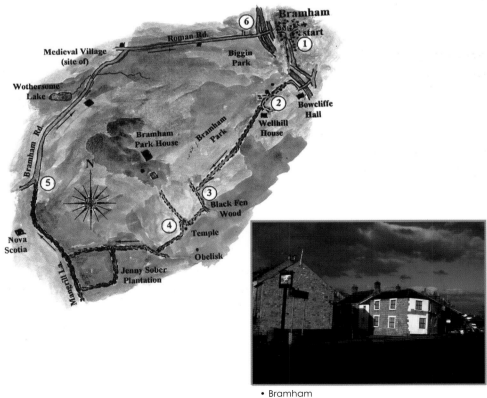

• Bramham

Directions

1. From the memorial cross in Bramham Square, go left along Bowcliffe Road to reach a 'T' junction on the outskirts of the village.

Bramham is an historic village, dating back to Roman times, with many Saxon, Norman and English Civil War connections. It lies alongside the busy A1(M) trunk road, just four miles south of Wetherby and eight miles west of York. Records from 1822 state: 'Bramham, a parish-town, in the wapentake of Barkston-Ash, liberty of St. Peter. Population, including Oglethorpe, 970, which being united form a township. The Church, is a vicarage, dedicated to All Saints, value - £6 7s 6d. (£6.37 in modern parlance). Patron, the Dean & Chapter of Christ Church College, Oxford.'

Cross the road to an enclosed footpath on the opposite side that leads towards the A1(M) before bearing left, parallel to the motorway, to reach a road bridge over it. On the far side turn immediately right alongside Bowcliffe Hall and follow the access drive to Bramham Park.

2. At a fork in the drive, alongside a fine old building known as The Priory, bear left (public footpath sign) towards Wellhill Farm, but just before the drive swings left towards farm buildings, go right on to a rough track.

This runs along the edge of fields with views to the right of Bramham Park House, a splendid Queen Anne mansion built in 1698 in the style of a Florentine villa of the 16th century. The idea was brought back from Italy by Robert Benson, 1st Lord Bingley, in 1679. It was planned as a summer home and a place where Benson could entertain his friends when Court and Parliament were in recess. It's now a little over 300 years since the house was built, but the descendants of Robert Benson still own and live at Bramham Park, a rare event in a land dogged by death-duties which have seen many a man forced to relinquish his family seat. The sumptuous rooms contain fine collections of furniture, porcelain and paintings, many of family members.

3. At a junction with a cross-track bear left and head towards Black Fen Wood, but just before reaching a white painted gate giving access to the woods, turn right along another track with the 18th century Round House Temple directly ahead.

This is a grade 1 listed building surrounded by a ditch and retaining wall on three sides and known as a ha-ha. Along one of the forest clearances radiating out from the grassy area surrounding the Temple, can be seen The Obelisk, a tall, elegant memorial pointing to the Yorkshire sky and erected by George Fox Lane, Lord Bingley, and Harriet Benson, his wife, in remembrance of their only son, Robert Fox Lane. With over 150 acres, visitors can spend a whole day exploring the lovely parkland and outstanding gardens here at Bramham Park. The gardens were laid out by Robert Benson in the thirty years following the completion of the house. The inspiration for the design was French and formal, but the manner in which it was adapted to the natural landscape is relaxed and entirely

English. They are almost unique in the country for being perhaps the only large-scale formal gardens to survive virtually unchanged from the early 18th century. The garden has superb vistas, lined by magnificent beech hedges, charming architectural features and soothing water cascades and ponds that create memorable reflections in their mirror surfaces.

4. Skirt round the Temple and proceed along the track. However, if you wish to visit Bramham Park House (see information for opening times) go right along the signposted footpath towards the house. At a junction with another track, in a belt of trees, go right to reach a fork in Jenny Sober Plantation, keep to the left branch which is now a grassy track that swings left to reach a junction with a broad farm track known as Mangrill Lane. Turn right along this and follow it out to a junction with Bramham Road.

5. Bear right along this, passing Wothersome Lake down to the left which is usually home to a small flock of wildfowl. Pass a small disused quarry before swinging right along Thorner Road at a road junction.

The fields to the left at this point were the site of the former medieval village of Wothersome, but apart from a few undulations in the ground, nothing remains of the buildings that once housed this Yorkshire community.

Continue along Thorner Road, which follows the line of an old Roman consular road that ran from the Roman fort at Camulodunum (near Huddersfield), through Calcaria (Tadcaster) and on to Eburacum (York). It was close to here that Sir Thomas Rokesby routed the Earl of Northumberland's forces. The Earl, the main protagonist in deposing Richard II and bringing Henry IV to the English throne, was also slain and his head carried on a stake in mock procession to London, where it was finally hung from the bridge.

6. Cross the A1(M) once more, but at a 'T' junction on the far side, turn left for 5yds. before crossing to a footpath on the opposite side of the motorway slip road. This descends to a flight of steps, which in turn lead down on to a cul-de-sac known as Tenter Hill. Go left, past the White Horse Inn and back to The Square in Bramham.

• The Temple, Bramham Park.   • Bramham sign on Thorner Rd.   • Bramham church.

Stoodley Pike

Hebden Bridge - Stoodley Pike Monument - Rochdale Canal & River Calder

Introduction

A cracking walk which climbs steeply out of Calderdale at first before easy paths and tracks lead across open moorland to what must be the finest viewpoint in the South Pennines; Stoodley Pike. The return leg is in sharp contrast to this as it follows the towpath which is squeezed in between the Rochdale Canal and the River Calder.

Points of interest

Hebden Bridge is a picturesque mill town with tiers of workers cottages clinging to the hillside above the river. Stoodley Pike Monument has a viewing balcony which affords the most expansive views over the West Riding hills while the Rochdale Canal, alive with boats and wildlife in the summer months, is a haven of peace and tranquillity in the short days of winter.

Information

Distance & time:	6.5 miles (10.5km). 3.5 - 4 hrs. approximately.
Start & finish:	Tourist Information Centre, Hebden Bridge. (Grid Ref: 992272)
Maps:	OS Outdoor Leisure 21. South Pennines 1:25 000.
Parking:	plentiful in Hebden Bridge.
Public Transport:	regular bus services from Halifax, Rochdale & Burnley. West Yorkshire Passenger Transport Tel: 01422 365985. Train services from Leeds, Halifax & Manchester. Contact Metro Tel: 0113 2457676
Refreshments:	Pubs and cafes in Hebden Bridge. Inn at Stubbing Wharf close to end of walk.
Tourist Information:	1 Bridge Gate, Hebden Bridge, West Yorks. HX7 8EX. Tel: 01422 843831.

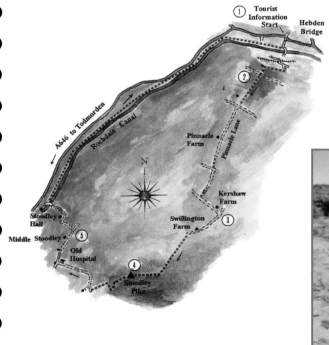

• The wintery walk to Stoodley Pike

Directions

1. From the Tourist Information Centre, cross the main A642 Halifax Road turning left then right into Holme Street, passing the Post Office on the left. At the end bear left then right over the Rochdale Canal, turning right on the far side to cross the Black Pit Aqueduct over the River Calder before climbing a flight of steps. At the top go right for a few yards then left to follow the road over the railway, continuing for a

further 100yds. before turning right up a rough tarmac track that swings left behind houses. After 80 yds. turn sharp right onto a grassy track that rises towards an isolated house, going left just before the house on an indistinct path alongside a wall which climbs steeply through Crow Nest Wood.

2. At the top of the wood negotiate a stone stile, cross a rough track and pass through a gate on the far side with a footpath sign to Pinnacle Lane and climb steadily through a series of fields, keeping the wall on the left. At the brow of the hill the days destination comes into view; Stoodley Pike, whilst to the rear there are fine views over Hebden Bridge and the Pennine Moors beyond.

This is a fine view point from which to study the geography of Hebden Bridge which started life as an insignificant settlement, cramped into a small patch of flat land between Hebden Water and the River Calder. However, during the Industrial Revolution, Hebden found itself ideally situated to exploit the energies of its rivers and streams and join other South Pennine towns by cashing in on the textile trade. Consequently the town expanded, but Calderdale has little flat land so the only way was upwards, with terraced cottages clinging tenuously to the hillsides. Today, these renovated buildings provide fine accommodation for Hebden's inhabitants and the town is enjoying a new boom as a tourist centre.

After crossing a lane, continue ahead along a farm track - Pinnacle Lane - for

approximately half a mile, with splendid views in all directions. At the end of the lane pass through a gate into a field, keeping in the same direction through this and another field to a gate leading onto a farm track. Turn left along the track, past Kershaw Farm, to a 'T' junction with another track.

- The Rochdale Canal at Hebden Bridge
- Snow encrusted walls snake over the Pennines

3. Go right along this track, past Swillington farm, to pass through a gate into a rough pasture. Continue ahead for a few yards to a footpath sign indicating 'Pennine way & Stoodley Pike', here bear left to follow a gently rising path across moorland to a ladder stile over a stone wall. On the far side go right, through a gap in a cross wall and continue up to the monument atop of Stoodley Pike.

The monument was originally erected here, at an altitude of 1,320ft. (402m), in 1815 to commemorate the surrender of Paris after the Napoleonic Wars. Unfortunately, lightning struck the first obelisk which eventually collapsed to be replaced by the present 125ft. high structure (complete with lightning conductor) in 1856. On the valley side of the monument, a doorway leads to a flight of steps which spiral gloomily through the interior before opening out onto a viewing balcony which circles the tower, affording the most wonderful views.

4. From the valley (north west) side of the monument, a steep zigzag path descends from the moor, heading for the eastern extremities of Todmorden. At the bottom of the moor climb a stile at the side of a gate onto a track which descends to join another track. Go right along this, past the Old Hospital which is now being converted to domestic dwellings, to a 'T' junction. Turn right along the lane which is initially metalled but soon becomes a rough track at a Private Road and Public Bridleway sign.

5. Shortly after passing the buildings of Middle Stoodley, turn left at a bridleway sign to Stoodley Glen. This tarmacadam lane descends steeply, swings sharp right by Stoodley Hall then continues down through woodland to the canal. Cross the canal into a car park, which once served Stoodley Mill, then turn sharp left to reach the bank of the canal.

This stretch of the Rochdale Canal, planned to link the Calder and Hebble Navigation at Sewerby Bridge to the Bridgewater Canal in Manchester, was opened in 1798, 32 years after the initial survey had been conducted. The main delays were caused by mill owners in the Calder Valley who thought that the water required to operate the canal; estimated at some 5_ million gallons per day, would jeopardise their livelihoods which relied on supplies from local rivers and streams. Rather ironic considering the canal was partly being built for their benefit!

In 1953 the canal was officially closed by the Rochdale Canal Company and many parts were filled in and bridges demolished. In 1974 the Rochdale Canal Society was formed and the mighty task of restoring the canal began. It is hoped that by the turn of the century, the whole navigation will once more be open.

Turn left here, beneath the bridge, to follow this attractive stretch of towpath, squeezed in between the canal and River Calder, all the way back to Hebden Bridge.

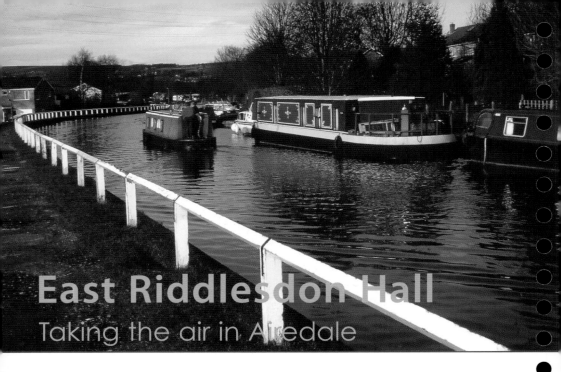

East Riddlesden Hall
Taking the air in Airedale

Bingley - Micklethwaite - East Morton - East Riddlesden Hall - Leeds & Liverpool Canal

Introduction

Despite the crowded nature of Airedale between Bingley and Keighley, where river, road, railway and canal are squeezed into the narrow confines of the valley bottom, mother nature still weaves her magical web. This walk samples some of the delights of the dale, including 17th century houses, a wonderfully restored canal, attractive villages and ancient field pathways.

Points of interest

The Leeds & Liverpool Canal was built between 1773 and 1819 in order to provide improved access between the industrial towns of Yorkshire and a desirable sea port. East Riddlesden Hall is one of several examples of a 'Halifax House' in the West Pennines, built for wealthy merchants. Numerous rock carvings on the moors that fringe this part of Airedale are signs of ancient occupation.

Information

Distance & time:	7.5 miles (12km) 3 - 3.5 hrs not including stops.
Start & finish:	Bingley Station car park (Grid Ref: 108392)
Maps:	OS Explorer 27 Lower Wharfedale and OS Explorer 288 Bradford & Huddersfield.
Parking:	See start & finish.
Public Transport:	Metro buses and trains from Leeds, Bradford and Skipton. Tel: 0113 245 7676.
Refreshments:	cafes, pubs and hotels in Bingley. Inn at Riddlesden. Cafe at East Riddlesden Hall.
Tourist Information:	2-4 West Lane, Haworth, Nr Keighley. BD22 8EF. Tel: 01535 642329
East Riddlesden Hall:	National Trust. For opening times and further information contact: East Riddlesden Hall Tel: 01535 607075

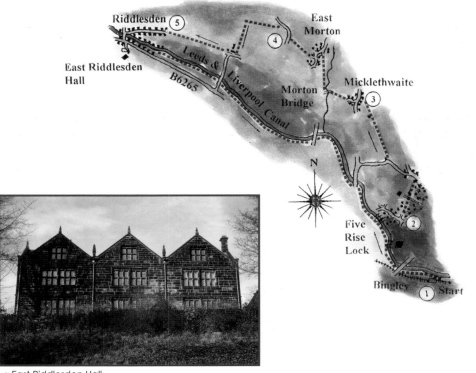

• East Riddlesdon Hall

Directions

1. Walk across the station car park, through a gap in the low wall onto the towpath of the Leeds and Liverpool canal and turn left along this, passing first Bingley Three Rise Lock then, one of the highlights of the whole navigation, Bingle Five Rise Lock.

Designed by John Longbotham of Halifax and built in 1774, the locks raise boats 59ft 2ins. over a distance of 320 ft. For anyone fancying a slightly longer walk, Leeds is 16 miles 2 furlongs away from here but Liverpool will probably need a little thinking about at 111 miles.

Cross the footbridge at the top of Five Rise Lock onto a narrow lane, turning right at the end into Beck Lane then, just before the next turning on the right, go left along a tarmac drive at the end of which is an iron kissing gate leading onto an enclosed footpath.

2. The path climbs steadily alongside well tended gardens before crossing the drive to Gawthorpe Hall which lies to the left.

This ancient dwelling, built in 1595, was once home to the local Lords of the Manor. In recent years it was divided to provide two homes but now serves again as originally intended; a single, private house.

Continue ahead along the enclosed path to eventually join Pinedale, a short section of road in a new housing development, where the continuation path lies directly ahead across another new road. This now rises more steeply before being directed to the left of houses and into a section of woodland, at the far end of which, a short flight of steps leads to a wooden pedestrian gate and the road. Turn left here, keeping left at the road junction into Greenhill Lane which descends quite steeply. At the left-hand bend, cross to an enclosed footpath at the right-hand side of a house and follow this into open country where the panorama steadily improves, with expansive views along the Aire Valley to the rolling hills of the Dales. After a pedestrian gate the path runs along the bottom of a short, open field, then right of farm buildings to join the farm drive, but where this swings left just beyond the farm, continue ahead over a stone stile right of a gate and follow the grassy field track into the village of Micklethwaite.

• The splendid Five Rise Lock on the Leeds & Liverpool Canal near Bingley.

• The monastic fish pond and one of the barns at East Riddlesden Hall.

3. Turn left at the road, skirting the village green, then, immediately in front of the Methodist Chapel, turn right along Beck Road then left alongside Beck Farm Barn, swinging right at the end of the buildings onto an enclosed footpath just right of the tarmac drive to Hollroyd Mill. The path eventually descends to Hebble Bride, a footbridge spanning Morton Beck, on the far side of which veer right to join a lane

on the outskirts of East Morton. Go left for 20yds. then cross into a cobbled yard and onto an enclosed footpath at the end of which is a pedestrian gate leading through another cobbled yard (Little Lane) onto Main Road. Turn left through the village and 100yds. past the telephone box, cross onto an unmade lane with a fish and chip shop and antiques

imporium on the left. Follow the unmade road round to the left, between houses, and immediately beyond High Fold turn right alongside mini-gardens to reach an enclosed footpath with iron railings on the left. The path runs alongside allotments before joining Street Lane which is followed to the right for approximately 200yds.

4. Just beyond a tarmac drive with iron gates on the left, go left through a field gate onto a field track and follow this through a gap in the wall ahead, turning right alongside the wall on the far side, and continue in this direction through fields. After a stone squeeze stile right of a gate, the path joins an enclosed track for a short distance, negotiates an

iron gate then crosses a short section of field to a gated stile leading onto Bury Lane. This is an enclosed track which is followed to the left, through a short section of field, then on down the continuation track to eventually join Carr Lane beside houses. Turn right along the road, continuing directly ahead at the left-hand bend onto South View, at the end of which is another enclosed footpath. After a wooden pedestrian gate the path runs along the bottom of a field, descends a short bank to cross How Beck then becomes a broad, enclosed path leading onto a road on the outskirts of Riddlesden.

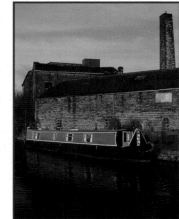

• Micklethwaite.
• A tranquil scene on the Leeds - Liverpool navigation near Bingley.
• Industry and leisure go hand-in-hand on the Leeds/Liverpool Canal.

5. Walk along the road, turning left at the bottom beside The Marqius of Granby, and over the canal swing bridge. The continuation walk goes left along the canal towpath all the way back to Bingley but to visit East Riddlesden Hall, continue down the road, crossing the B6265 at the pedestrian lights, with the Hall directly ahead.

This is a charming 17th Century West Riding yeoman's house, built for the wealthy Halifax clothier, James Murgatroyd. Influential merchants are responsible for a number of similarly constructed houses in this part of Yorkshire, most being based around a hall with cross-wings, and as such they have become known as 'Halifax Houses'. The Hall has fine displays of plasterwork, embroideries, pewter and Yorkshire oak furniture. One of the highlights of a visit is the splendid timber framed Great Barn which houses a number of traditional agricultural implements.

A serene scene along the Leeds & Liverpool canal

Cannon Hall
cannons a blazing

Cawthorne - Cawthorne Park - High Hoyland - Deffer Wood - Cannon Hall & Country Park

Introduction

A nice easy walk through the rolling countryside to the west of Barnsley with a pleasing combination of streams, ornamental lakes, villages, dark woodland, open fields and historic buildings at Cannon Hall and Cawthorne.

Points of interest

Cawthorne is an attractive village with a fine old church, interesting museum and welcoming pub. Cannon Hall is a beautiful 18th. century country house with lovely gardens, a visitor centre, museum, shop and cafe. The Country Park covers approximately 70 acres and encompasses lakes, streams, landscaped parkland and an interactive working farm.

Information

Distance & time:	6 miles (9.7km) 2.5-3 hours.
Start & finish:	Village Green, Cawthorne.
Map:	OS Outdoor Leisure 1 The Peak District Dark Peak Area
Parking:	roadside parking in Cawthorne.
Public Transport:	buses from Barnsley and Huddersfield. Tel: Traveline 01709 515151
Refreshments:	pubs at Cawthorne and High Hoyland. Cafe at Cannon Hall.
Tourist Information:	56 Eldon Street, Barnsley, South Yorks. S70 2JL. Tel: 01226 206757
Cannon Hall:	For opening times and further information contact: Cannon Hall Tel: 01226 790270

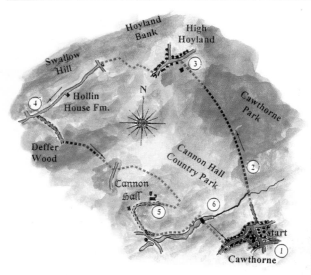

• Pansies brighten up the winter gardens at Cannon Hall.

Directions

1. Walk towards the village, passing to the left of the popular Spencer Arms then just beyond the Post Office go right along Darton Road.

The earliest record of Cawthorne is to be found in the Domesday Book which states that the manor was 'three miles long and two broad', but the name is much older than this and translates from Old English as 'bare thorn bush'. As with many ancient parishes, the focal point of the village is the church and this is the case here, with cottages clustered around the 13th century All Saints and the rest of the buildings radiating out along roads that old documents refer to as 'The Lanes'.

Immediately beyond the Methodist Chapel go left onto an enclosed footpath that descends to a stile, cross and walk along the left edge of a field to reach a footbridge spanning Cawthorne Dike then continue in the same direction, following the footpath sign for High Hoyland, and climbing gently towards Cawthorne Wood.

2. The path through the woods is obvious and fringed by deciduous trees that mask a denser and darker growth of coniferous woodland before exiting into a field.

The area around Cawthorne was once heavily industrialised with quarries, ironstone workings and coal mines scarring the land, but centuries of horse drawn and tractor pulled plough have covered the blemishes, leaving the land gently undulating and verdant. People are frequently surprised at the beauty of the countryside to the west of Barnsley which has, in the past, been labelled as a land of slag heaps and pit head winding gear. Things have changed!

Proceed up the right-hand side of two fields with a wall and wood to the right and fine views over the rolling countryside towards the moors of the Peak District to the left, before following an obvious footpath through Margery Wood.

This is quite a pleasing blend of deciduous and coniferous woodland with good breaks between the trees, allowing light to reach flowering plants and grasses which flourish in this sheltered environment and so creating a much more diverse habitat for wildlife.

Pass through a gap in a wall on the far side of the wood and bear left round the edge of a field to join a surfaced track leading into High Hoyland.

• The Spencer Arms at the start of the walk, Cawthorne.

3. Go left through this attractive village, passing the recently refurbished Cherry Tree public house on the right, then just beyond a 'Y' fork go right opposite a public footpath sign, up steps into a field and walk up the right edge of this. Pass through a gap in a low wall at the far end onto a broad, tree lined path and go left along this for 70 yards to an awkward stile on the right leading into a sloping field.

Bear right across this to a stile on the far side where a steep footpath descends between stately trees growing on the western slopes of Hoyland Bank. Climb a stile at the bottom of the bank, bear left round the edge of a field with the massive Emley Moor transmitter dominating the skyline to the right then, towards the end of the field, veer right round buildings to reach an iron kissing gate leading onto a road and cross into Hollin House Lane.

4. Opposite the junction with Wheatley Hill Lane go left (footpath sign) down an enclosed track between fields to a stile leading into Deffer Wood. Go left along a well made forestry track, bear right at a junction with another track then cross a track onto a narrow footpath through a belt of rhododendron bushes to a stile leading into a field. Walk along its right edge, cross a quiet lane into another field then bear slightly left across this to a stile on the far side and go right along the top edge of this to reach a stile beside a gate. Once over keep ahead alongside iron railings skirting the adventure playground at Home Farm to a stile and steps leading into the grounds of Cannon Hall Country Park.

The beautifully landscaped parkland covers over 70 acres with extensive grassy areas, ornamental lakes, large stands of trees colourful flower beds and a lovely walled garden.

Follow the grassy footpath skirting a ditch and ha-ha to a footbridge leading into the

gardens of Cannon Hall and proceed through fine trees, flower borders and past the walled garden towards the house, the main entrance to which is on the north side.

• The ornamental lakes, Cannon Hall Country Park.
• Cannon Hall

5. There was probably a dwelling standing on this site in Saxon times but no trace exists today other than we know the Manor of Cawthorne was held by a Saxon called Ailric. The estate changed hands many times until the late 1600's when it became the property of the Spencer's, a family who had a profound influence on the area and who remained here for the next 300 years when the property was

acquired by Barnsley County Borough Council. Much of the palatial house that stands here today was either built or modified during the 18th century and is a characteristic example of a Georgian country house which now houses a fine museum with extensive collections of furniture, glass, paintings and pottery. The fascinating history of the 13th/18th Royal Hussars (Queen Mary's own) can also be traced here from Waterloo to Bosnia.

After visiting continue along the path, bearing left down towards the car park and passing the Deer Shed on the right.

This is unusually ornate considering its function as shelter for deer and probably cattle too. It has highly decorative arched windows embellished with tracery and crude carvings with five massive yew trunks supporting the central bay.

Bear left across the car park towards the ornamental lakes and go left alongside these with large flocks of geese and ducks acting as escorts providing you have the right credentials - supplies of stale bread and cakes!

6. Cross the lakes via the arched Palladian Bridge and follow a surfaced path on the far side to eventually join a road on the outskirts of Cawthorne. At a 'T' junction go left along Tivy Dale, past a pleasing mixture of old and not so old dwellings, to reach the Victoria Jubilee Museum on the right.

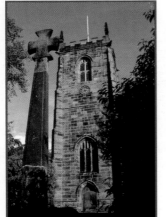

Founded in 1884 by the Reverend Charles Tiplady Pratt who encouraged the young members of his parish to become interested in wildlife. Collections of birds eggs, wild flowers, fossils, shells and grasses were made, astronomy and the weather studied and winter lectures known as 'penny readings' given.

Walk up steps at the side of the museum onto a grassy footpath to the rear of the building, go right along this to a junction with a path in front of the church yard and turn left along this to reach All Saints Church. Pass to the right of the church and bear left past the Church Hall, once a school, into Church Lane to return to the centre of the village close to the Spencer Arms.

• The Deer Shed, Cannon Hall.
• All Saints Church, Cawthorne.

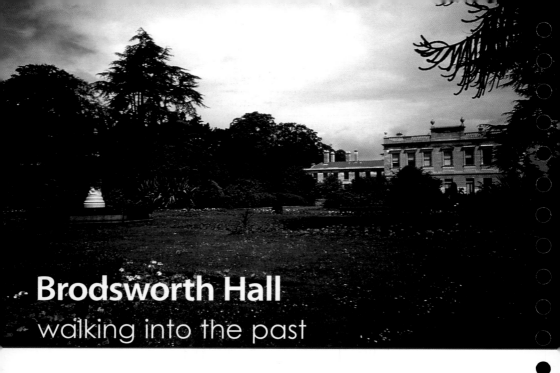

Brodsworth Hall
walking into the past

Hooton Pagnel - Hampole Wood - Pickburn - Brodsworth Hall - Brodsworth

Introduction

A gentle walk through lush agricultural land on the borders between South and West Yorkshire. It starts from one of the prettiest villages in the county, enters open countryside along medieval trackways, then visits the magnificent Brodsworth Hall, a building which has changed little for well over 100 years.

Points of interest

Hooton Pagnel, first mentioned in the Domesday Book, is a lovely unspoiled village of mellow stone cottages based around the medieval hall and church. Brodsworth Hall, surrounded by 17 acres of garden, is a fascinating building, once described as 'the most complete example of a Victorian Country House in England'.

Information

Distance & time:	7.25 miles (11.7km) 4hrs approx. not including stops.
Start & finish:	The Post Office, Hooton Pagnel.
Map:	OS Explorer 278 Sheffield & Barnsley and OS Explorer 279 Doncaster.
Parking:	discreet roadside parking in village or start of Broad Balk.
Public Transport:	Mainline Service 211 & West Riding Service 497/498 from Doncaster. Tel: 01709 515151
Refreshments:	cafe at Brodsworth Hall.
Tourist Information:	Central Library, Waterdale, Doncaster. DN1 3JE. Tel: 01302 734309
Brodsworth Hall:	English Heritage. For opening times and further information contact: Brodsworth Hall Tel: 01302 722598

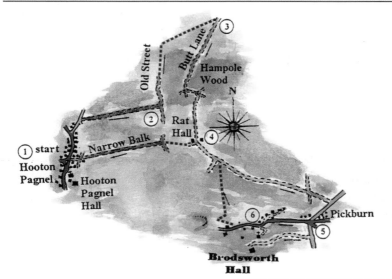

• Brodsworth Hall

Directions

1. From the Post Office in Hooton Pagnel turn right through the village in a northerly direction, past honey coloured stone cottages nestling beneath orange, pantile roofs.

This is one of the most attractive villages in the county and one which has changed little with the passage of time. It originated as an estate village based around the medieval hall which still stands at the southern end of the village and next to the lovely All Saints' Church. The first recorded mention of the village is found in the Domesday Book where it is called 'Hotone' or, 'the town on the hill'. The second part of the name is derived from Ralph de Pagnel, a later lord of the manor. In the centre of the village lies the old Butter Cross and beneath it the 'pound', an area in which cattle were once impounded.

At a 'Y' fork on the outskirts of the village bear right along North Field Road for 200yds. to reach the entrance to Broad Balk on the right. Pass through the white painted gates and walk along this broad track which is part of the Cusworth Cycle Trail.

2. The 'Balks' are remnants from medieval strip farming days. They were lanes running parallel with the strip enclosures, allowing farm carts easy access between the village and the fields.

At the end of the track go left along Lound Lane, another ancient track, which passes alongside Hampole Wood on the right. At the end of the wood the 'lane' joins Old Street, a footpath with hedges on either side, festooned with wildflowers during spring and summer. 20yds. beyond a junction with Lenny Balk, the most northerly of the medieval tracks, go right at a public bridleway sign and along the right edge of a field.

The views now open out across the northern extremities of South Yorkshire and on into West Yorkshire with the dark spine of the Pennines just visible on the western horizon.

The path initially runs alongside a hedge, then across an open section of field before rejoining the hedge. Cross into a second field and continue to a junction with a field track known as Butts Lane.

3. Turn right along the track towards Hampole Wood which is entered by a yellow waymarker. The woods provide pleasant shade on sunny days compared to the

exposure of the fields. At a crossroads of tracks 75yds. into the woods, turn left to reach another crossroad, this time turning right alongside an area recently planted with oak, beech and birch, to emerge from the trees on the edge of fields. Bear left round the field and on along a broad, grassy track towards the farm buildings at Rat Hall.

• The attractive 'Corner Cottage', Hooton Pagnel.

4. Pass through the farmyard (noisy but restrained dogs) onto the main farm drive and go left along this for 300yds to where the drive swings to the right. Continue directly ahead here along a hedged in track which soon runs across broad, open fields with views towards Doncaster and with the spire of Bently church prominent ahead. Continue for three-quarters of a mile but just before a stand of trees known as Church Plantation, leave the main track and proceed directly ahead, passing to the right of the wood to reach the road on the outskirts of Pickburn. Turn right along the road to a complex 5-way road junction and cross with care onto the road signposted to 'Brodsworth Hall'.

5. To visit the hall, walk along the road for 200yds. then turn right along the entrance drive.

One of England's most beautiful Victorian country houses and one which has remained almost in a time warp since the 1860's. Designed by the little known Italian, Chevalier Casentini and executed by an equally unknown architect, Philip Wilkinson, Brodsworth amply fulfilled its role as a grand residence for the owner, Charles Thellusson. After World War I however, spiraling costs meant that sections of the house were shut down, along with their contents, and the gardens became overgrown. When English Heritage acquired the hall, their policy was to preserve the faded Victorian grandeur in as much an undisturbed way as possible so that visitors can now virtually step back in time! To continue the walk, return to the road junction at Pickburn and go left along the Hooton Pagnel road, passing through the village of Brodsworth. To visit the lovely church of St. Michael and All Saints, go left up the signposted drive after quarter of a mile. Brodsworth is an ancient, unspoiled village mentioned in the Domesday Book.

• The magnificent south front of Brodsworth hall.
• The 'Butter Cross', Hooton Pagnel.
• Across the rooftops, Hooten Pagnal

It is known that a church existed in the area as long ago as Saxon times, but the present church dates from the Norman period. In recent years the church has suffered from mining subsidence and was swathed in scaffolding before repair work could be funded in order to restore it to its former glory.

After visiting the church, return to and continue along the road, this time along the footpath on the left-hand side.

6. After 350 yds. cross to climb a stile on the opposite side of the road into a field, turning left past a barn and alongside the boundary wall of the village hall before climbing a stile over a rustic fence. Descend to join a rough track which rises up the field to reach a public footpath sign after 50yds. and go right onto a subsidiary track which skirts a disused quarry. On entering a field, walk alongside the right hedge then on along a broad field track to a junction with the track from Rat Hall. Turn left along this, skirting to the left of the farm and onto a field-side footpath before crossing Lound Lane onto Narrow Balk. At the end of Narrow Balk go left for a few yards along Back Lane, then right along a tarmac lane and beneath a wonderful canopy of copper beech trees back into Hooton Pagnel.

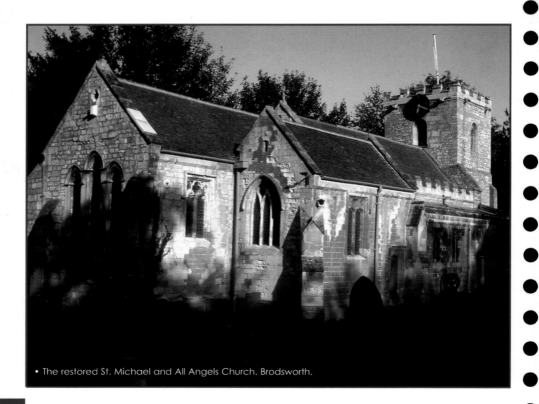

• The restored St. Michael and All Angels Church. Brodsworth.

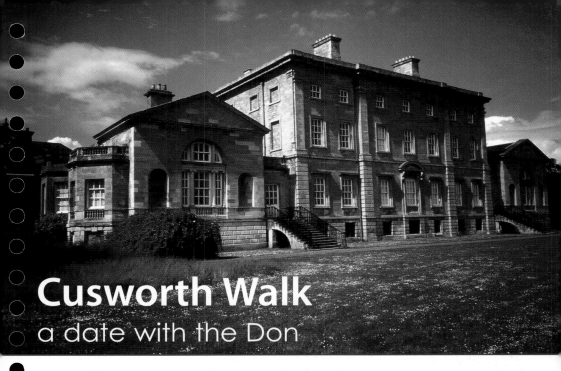

Cusworth Walk
a date with the Don

Sprotbrough - Cusworth Park - Cusworth Hall - Richmond Hill - River Don - Sprotbrough

Introduction

An easy walk through the rich farmland 10 the west of Doncaster, starting from the lovely village of Sprotbrough then on through Cusworth Country Park to the splendid Cusworth Hall which now houses the Museum of South Yorkshire Life. The return section follows a section of dismantled railway line before joining one of South Yorkshire's most important waterways, the River Don.

Points of interest

Sprotbrough is a lovely old estate village regarded by many as being one of the most attractive in South Yorkshire. The magnificent limestone building of Cusworth Hall, once the home of me Wrightson family, now houses the Museum of South Yorkshire Life. Some of the grounds of the Hall now form part of Cusworth Country Park. The River Don is one of the areas principal waterways and one that has played an important role in the industrial development of South Yorkshire.

Information

Distance & time:	5.5 miles (9.3km) 2.5 - 3 hours. Not including stops.
Start & finish:	Sprotbrough Bridge.
Maps:	OS Explorer 279 Doncaster.
Parking:	small car park to west of Sprotbrough Bridge (road to Cadeby).
Public Transport:	Service 44 from Doncaster and Service 74 Bolton upon Dearne - Mexbrough. Tel: 01709 515151
Refreshments:	pubs in Sprotbrough. Cafe at Cusworth Hall.
Tourist Information:	Central Library, Waterdale, Doncaster, DN1 3JE. Tel: 01302 734309.
Cusworth Hall:	For opening times and further information contact: Cusworth Hall Tel: 01302 782342

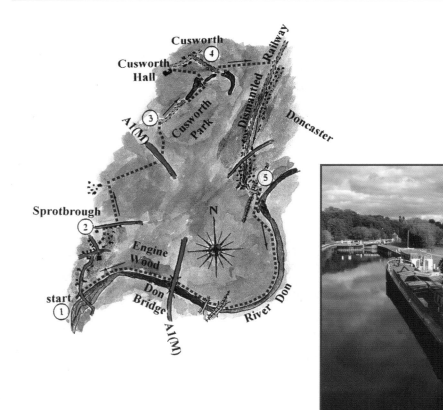

• Boats moored at Sprotbrough Locks.

Directions

1. From Sprotbrough Bridge walk up Boat Lane into the village.

Prior to the building of Sprotbrough Bridge, a ferry used to ply across the Don at this point, shuttling passengers between Sprotbrough and Warmsworth on the south side of the river. The little building on the north side of the bridge is the old Toll House but the payment of tolls ceased in 1888.

At the junction by the village green go right towards the church of St. Mary.

There are a number of old cottages scattered around the village and until 1926 there was a rather fine hall, owned by the Copley family, but this was demolished and much of the estate is now covered with modern housing.

It's not known how long a village has stood here, but defined parish boundaries and various scraps of evidence, including an Anglo-Saxon cross shaft, would suggest that there has been a settlement here well before the Norman conquests. The village is recorded in the Domesday Book as 'Sprotesburg', but there is no mention of a church. This is no proof that a place of worship did not exist here prior to 1086 however as many churches were built before this date yet omitted from the records. The present church is thought to be about 825 years old and is a splendid limestone building with an unusual sundial on the south face of the tower.

Follow the road round to the left, passing the village Post Office, to a stile over a wall on the right after 75 yards and bear diagonally left across a playing field with the "Ivanhoe' beyond.

Sir Walter Scott is reputed to have lived at Boat Farm in the lower part of the village whilst writing the novel 'Ivanhoe', hence the name of the pub.

Go through an iron gate on the far side and turn left along a surfaced drive.

2. At a junction with Melton Road turn right for 150 yards then cross with care onto a public footpath running through the middle of a field. At a junction with a broad farm track just right of a barn, turn right, continuing ahead on a good footpath when the track ends to reach a pedestrian tunnel beneath the A1(M). Once through bear diagonally left to a footbridge over a drainage channel, turn immediately right on the far side then go left alongside trees on the edge of Cusworth Country Park. After a short distance the path swings right, away from the trees, with the magnificent limestone edifice of Cusworth Hall directly ahead, to a junction with a broad track.

• Sprotbrough weir

3. Go right along this. Passing to the right of one of the ornamental lakes in the park and at the end go left over two bridges on to a surfaced footpath between fine mature trees that leads up to Cusworth Hall, the public entrance to which is on the north side of the building.

Despite its graceful lines, opulent size and magnificent outlook, this stately pile does not have walls dripping with Rembrandts, Turners or Titians; floors ankle deep in the most lush of Flemish carpets; tables decorated with the finest tea services or rooms adorned with furniture from the very best of European cabinet makers. Instead it has displays of Doncaster's sweet manufacturers, photographs of life down the pit, a room full of old TVs and radios, a model railway layout, smoothing irons, butter churns, dolly maids and what every stately home should have in its lobby, a Co-op bicycle complete with basket! For this the home of the Museum of South Yorkshire Life. Of course this has not always been the case. The present building was built as a manor house by William Wrightson in the mid 1700's, replacing a smaller, less ostentatious dwelling that he felt did not suitably display his wealth and importance. Over the years the Hall passed from entailed heir to entailed heir until 1952 when the childless Robert Cecil Battie-Wrightson died of a cerebral haemorrhage. The next in line was his sister Barbara, but Robert's demise incurred heavy death duties assessed at £280,000, a staggering amount for the time. Securities to the value of a quarter million pounds were cashed but in order to raise the shortfall, Barbara decided to auction the Hall's contents and one of the most famous sales of this century ensued, lasting nine days and raising £36.000.

Following the sale, Barbara was advised to dispose of the Hall as soon as possibly due to the prohibitive maintenance costs. Some of the ideas put forward for the Hall's future use included converting it into a home for lonely folk, using it as a prison, establishing a Borstal Institution, converting it into a hospital, developing a zoo and even demolishing the whole structure. Eventually, in 1961, the building and grounds were purchased by Doncaster Rural District Council for £7,500 and Cusworth Hall Museum opened in 1967. In 1974, under the ownership of the newly created Metropolitan Borough Council, the theme of the museum became 'South Yorkshire Life' and since this time it has, under the leadership of several curators, attempted to illustrate aspects of life in the area from the last 200 years.

After visiting turn right along a broad surfaced drive that leads through iron gates and into the village of Cusworth. This takes you past some fine old buildings including Church Cottage and Cusworth Glebe which stand on the site of the original Hall.

• A motorcycle event at Cusworth Hall.

4. Despite recent expansion, this part of Cusworth still retains much of the character of the original estate village with some attractive 17th and 18th century limestone cottages nestled into a south facing hillside and overlooking the Don Valley. Such is the charm of these cottages that many refer to it as 'a little piece of the Cotswolds here in Yorkshire'.

50 yards beyond the Orthodox Church turn right into Orchard Lane, swing left at the bottom between cottages and a pond and through a set of barriers then, at a 'Y' fork a little further on keep right along a surfaced track At a 'T" junction with another track go right and at a cross-roads of tracks go nght again, following the 'Cusworth Cycle Trail' sign, now along a dismantled railway line which is followed for three quarters of a mile. Just before a footbridge spanning the line go left up a flight of steps, turn right at the top then immediately left on to a raised footpath that leads to a footbridge over a functional railway line. Once across go left along a broad track and at the far end of a field bear right down a bank to reach the River Don.

5. Turn right alongside the Don, eventually joining a footpath along the top of a raised flood bank that circumnavigates a large loop in the river.

The rivers of Yorkshire have been an important means of transport since the earliest settlements and often determined the location and development of cities, towns and villages. However the Don, or Dun as it was originally known, was a bit of a disaster as far as transport was concerned until an Act in 1726 permitted its partial canalisation and improvement along the valley towards Sheffield. Prior to this, boats relied on seasonal rains in the Pennines and high tides backing up the Ouse and along the Don and even then, Doncaster was the head of navigation. Once improved however, the river and associated canal network played a major part in the industrial development of South Yorkshire.

The footpath passes beneath Don Bridge which carries the A1(M) high above the river before running alongside Sprotbrough Locks and back to Sprotbrough Bridge.

• Cusworth village, 'A little piece of the Cotswolds here in Yorkshire'.

• The river Don

Sheffield's industrial waterways

Victoria Quays – Sheffield & Tinsley Canal – Meadowhall – River Don – Victoria Quays

Introduction

This exploration of Sheffield's two most important waterways, the River Don and the Sheffield & Tinsley Canal, can be started from several places, including car parks, bus stops and supertram stops at Don Valley Stadium, Tinsley and Meadowhall Shopping Centre. The walk is almost flat, with no ascents or descents of note and much of the way is accessible for wheelchairs.

Information

Distance & time:	8 miles (13 km). 4 - 4.5 hrs approx. not including stoping.
Start & finish:	Victoria Quays, Sheffield. (A short walk from city centre).
Maps:	OS Explorer 278 Sheffield & Barnsley, or A-Z Street Atlas or map of Five Weirs Way available from Tourist Information.
Parking:	Pay & display car parks at Victoria Quays. Free car parks at Don Valley and Meadowhall.
Public Transport:	Buses and trains into Sheffield from most parts of the region. Closest supertram stop to Victoria Quays – Commercial St. Tel: 01709 515151 for all enquiries.
Refreshments:	Several pubs along the way, cafes and restaurants at Meadowhall, café and hotel at Victoria Quays.
Tourist Information:	1 Tudor Square, Sheffield. S1 2LA. Tel: 0114 2211900.

• Victoria Quays and the start of the walk.

Directions

1. From the cobbled courtyard at Victoria Quays, go left past the beautifully refurbished canalside arches, that now house a range of retail and service outlets, to join the towpath of the Sheffield & Tinsley Canal.

Opened in 1819, with a ceremony attended by nearly 60,000 people, the Sheffield & Tinsley Canal became a functional part of the Sheffield & South Yorkshire Navigation, linking the land-locked city to the sea. By 1968 the canal had been designated a 'Remainder Waterway' and although some trade did continue up to the early 1970's, the waterway lapsed into disrepair. Lock systems rotted, the canal bank began to crumble, water stagnated and the whole area became most unwelcoming.

In 1992 the Sheffield Development Corporation (SDC) and British Waterways put forward a masterplan for the redevelopment of 30 acres of land in and around the old canal basin. This was in conjunction with an £80 million Government assisted scheme to regenerate in all, 2,000 acres of derelict land in the Lower Don Valley. Phase one began in July 1993 when the basin was drained and repair work started. By December '94, the basin was refilled with a staggering 20 million gallons of water. The weekend of 6 - 8 May 1995 saw another opening ceremony on the Sheffield & Tinsley Canal with an even larger crowd than the first time witnessing the event and the re-christening of the old basin - Victoria Quays.

This regenerated area is once again playing a vibrant part in Sheffield's present and future. The Straddle Warehouse, so called because it sat astride the canal and allowed waterborne goods to be hoisted into the building through trap doors in the floor, now provides 20,000 sq. ft of unique and prestigious office space. (I hope the contractors secured the floor!)

The Terminal and Grain Warehouses now house a pub/restaurant and living

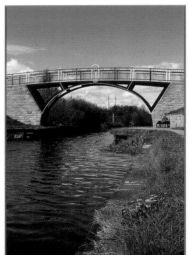

accommodation with the huge grain hoppers being retained as a very impressive and unusual feature. Sheaf Works, the first in Sheffield to dispense with waterpower and turn over to steam, has also been sensitively restored.

2. Continue along the towpath, first on the left-hand side of the canal, then on the right to reach Bacon Lane Bridge. Many of Sheffield's industrial heritage sites are visible from the canal side, including an original crucible chimney stack near Bacon Lane Bridge and close to where Benjamin Huntsman invented crucible steel making.

• The Sheffield & Tinsley Canal.

The canal eventually passes Stadium Moorings, with the futuristic towers of Don Valley International Stadium just beyond. This is the venue for major athletics and music events and the home of Sheffield Eagles Rugby League F.C. A little further along the canal is Sheffield Arena, one of the UK's top music venues and the home of the extremely successful Sheffield Steelers Ice Hockey team.

3. Just beyond here, climb onto the footbridge that spans the canal and tram lines, but half way across, go right to rejoin the towpath on the opposite side. This soon leads to Tinsley Top Locks and Marina.

The most numerous vessels on the navigation were massive sailing barges called 'Humber Keels'. They were known as Sheffield size and very distinctive, being 61ft 6ins. long, 15ft 3ins. wide with a blunt, rounded fore and aft and a single mast sheeted with two square sails. The 'Dorothy Pax' (now being restored at Sheffield Basin and soon to be on display,) is a typical example of one of these vessels.

Note the milepost plaque on lock 4 which commemorates the December 1940 Blitz when German bombs fell here, bursting the canal and demolishing the old Tinsley Lock house. Tinsley Marina now provides important moorings and a leisure destination for boaters. There are short and long term quality moorings, toilet and fuel points and landscaped walkways for visitors.

4. Just before reaching the M1 viaduct, go left at a waymarker indicating the Five Weirs Way, cross a footbridge and follow the red tarmac walkway alongside the road and past Meadowhall shopping complex.

This has proven to be a phenomenally successful venture, with 270 shops and over 30 million visitors a year. It was built on the site of Sheffield's mightiest steel plant, Hadfields East Heclia, which closed shortly after having worked through the 1981 steelworkers' strike.

Continue following signs for the Five Weirs Way, which now runs above the River Don and past the first of the weirs, Hadfields Weir, originally built in the 17th century to power cutler wheels. Proceed towards the buildings of Sheffield Forgemasters where the path swings

left above Brightside Weir, which has been in existence since 1328. Pass beneath an ornate archway, indicating the Five Weirs Way, cross Gairbrook Street, then Carbrook Hall Road, but just before reaching the A6109, bear right along the red tarmac walkway once more.

• The suspended walkway above the River Don near Wicker.

5. Cross Hawke Street and go right to reach a cycle barrier and footpath just beyond Bold Street, which leads back to the River Don. The footpath runs along the left bank of the river initially, then the right to reach Newhall Road. Cross the road bridge over the river to rejoin the footpath, now along the left bank once more.

The Lower Don Valley and the east end of Sheffield is now unrecognisable from that of 20 years ago. Thankfully the gross pollution of air, land and water is a thing of the past and from the industrial wasteland of the 80's has arisen a futuristic business, commercial and leisure complex. Reminders of the City's industrial past are still visible from the river, which is once again a clean waterway that attracts a plethora of wildlife.

Cross Stevenson Road, pass beneath another ornate arch and join a section of unsurfaced footpath that runs past Sanderson Weir.

This weir dates from about 1580 and was constructed on the orders of the Lord of the Manor, George Talbot, 6th Earl of Shrewsbury, but best known as the husband of Bess of Hardwick. He was also one of the leading industrialists of the Elizabethan Age, with interests in iron, coal and lead. The weir was built to provide power for two iron forges, known as the Upper and Nether Attercliffe Forges, each having its own goyt, or water channel, which took water from the weir to the water wheels. This area was once known as the 'hammer ground' because of the number of forges operating in the area.

6. Cross the East Coast Road Bridge and on the opposite side pass through a pair of ornate stone gateposts.

These gateposts came from the Spear & Jackson Aetna Works, which were demolished in 1991. The walk now runs along the right bank of the river and through an area known as Royds Mills. This is probably a local pronunciation of the name 'Rhodes', the family who ran three cutting wheels, a corn mill and a farm here in the 16th century.

Pass beneath the next bridge.

This is the Washford Bridge, originally built in 1789 to take the turnpike road from Sheffield to Tinsley Canal Wharf. The walk now enters Salmon Pastures, an area once covered by slagheaps from the Duke of Norfolk's coke ovens but now reclaimed and a refuge for wildlife. Urban foxes are not uncommon here, rabbits abound and the occasional hedgehog and water vole are spotted. Little grebe and grey heron share the river with numerous coots, moorhen and mallard and even cormorants and kingfishers are frequently seen. This is quite a juxtaposition in this land-locked heart of an industrial city.

• The old Baltic Works near Bacon Lane Bridge

Continue on to the next weir, Burton Weir, with the ornate ironwork of Norfolk Bridge just beyond. Bear right here, away from the Don to a junction of one of the city's old cobbled streets, Warren Street and turn left along this. At the end go left along Leverson Street, cross Norfolk Bridge then take the first turning on the right, Effingham Street, to eventually walk alongside the River Don once more and past Walk Mill Weir, built before 1581 to power a 'walk' or fulling mill.

7. Immediately before the railway viaduct, turn right into Sussex Street to reach a magnificent suspended footbridge above the Don, which takes the walker beneath the Wicker Viaduct.

The latter was built in 1849 to carry the Sheffield and Lincolnshire railway, Victoria Station and hotel. The area on the far side of the bridge is known as Wicker or 'Bailliwick', an important meeting point ever since Sheffield became a town. In 1112, a Norman castle was constructed on the high point over to the right where Castle Markets are currently being reconstructed. Being the closest flat land to the castle, the Wicker was used for archery practice, various tournaments, livestock markets and even witch ducking, while slaughter houses, or 'shambles', were set up beneath the castle walls. In 1827, the cattle market, having outgrown the Wicker, moved across the river to Black Street Bridge, an area still known today as 'Smithfield's'.

During the 18th century, the growth of Sheffield's cutlery trade led to the construction of numerous workshops and factories driven by waterwheels fed by Wicker Weir, but once steam was adopted, the whole of the riverside area in Wicker became enveloped in steelworks. So great was the pressure on land that many of the factories were built right out over the river on cast iron stilts.

At Lady's Bridge go left along the road, cross the access road to the Victoria Hotel and Furnival Road, then bear left through the archway leading back to Victoria Quays.

• Tinsley Basin and Marina.
• Supertram arrives at Tinsley.

113

Wortley Top Forge & Hall

Upper Don Valley - Wortley Park - Wortley Hall - Wortley Top Forge

Introduction

The River Don rises on the eastern moors of the Peak District National Park and flows in a roughly westerly direction through Sheffield and Doncaster before confluenceng with the Humber. It is hard to imagine how this sparkling waterway, as it flows near Wortley, was once the focal point of the British iron and steel industry. This lovely walk explores a section of the upper Don Valley, passes through Wortley Park with its fine Hall and also gives an opportunity to visit one of the few remaining iron forges that once pounded away in this area.

Points of interest

Wortley is an attractive village set astride the A629. It has an excellent pub, good café, a lovely church and fine views over the surrounding countryside. Wortey Hall was the original home of the Wortley family but has now been transformed into a fine hotel and conference centre. Wortley Top Forge is an excellent example of a 17th century iron works that is now an industrial museum.

Information

Distance & time:	5.5 miles (8.4km). 3 - 3.5 hrs. approximately.
Start & finish:	Cote Green Car Park. (off Finkle Street Lane, 1 mile west of Wortley.)
Maps:	OS Outdoor Leisure 1 The Peak District Dark Peak area or OS Explorer 278 Sheffield & Barnsley.
Parking:	See start.
Public Transport:	Buses to Wortley and Thurgoland from Barnsley, Penistone & Sheffield. Tel: 01709 515151.
Refreshments:	Café at Wortley, pubs in Thurgoland & Wortley.
Tourist Information:	46 Eldon Street, Barnsley. S70 2JL. Tel: 01226 206757. 1 Tudor Square, Sheffield. S1 2LA. Tel: 0114 201 1011.
Wortley Top Forge:	For opening times and further information contact: Wortley Top Forge Tel: 0114 2887576.

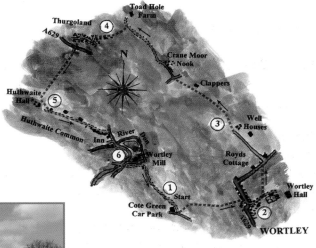

• Terraced cottages, Wortley.

Directions

1. From the car park bear right, past Cote Green Farm which offers livery for horses and accommodation for riders who are attempting the Trans Pennine Trail on horseback. The trail, which is designed for walkers, cyclists and riders, makes use of the dismantled railway line just below the car park and runs from Hull on the east coast to Southport on the west coast. At a junction with the road go left for 10yds to an iron kissing-gate on the left, giveing access to a paved footpath. This climbs steadily between and through fields as it heads towards Wortley, alighting in the village alongside the splendid church of St Leanard.

The name Wortley is Anglo-Saxon and means 'a clearing for growing crops'. In the Domesday Book it is recorded as 'waste', following severe ravaging by the Norman's. The village was largely rebuilt between 1830 and 1850 and there are a number of attractive houses that date from this period. The church of St Leanard, whose square tower dominates the skyline in this area, is built on 13th century foundations but largely dates from the mid 1700's. Opposite the church is the Wortley Arms, a well-known hostelry that serves excellent beer and food.

Cross the A629 with care, bear right on the opposite side past cottages, then take the first turning on the left, passing Wortley Post Office and café on the right and following signs to Wortley Hall.

2. At a fork in the road, in front of a fine mature tree with a wrap-around bench, veer left, between the entrance gateposts to the hall and walk down the access drive.

Wortley Hall is the ancestral home of the Wortley family, Earls of Wharncliffe. The earliest recording being Alnus de Wortley, mentioned in the Pipe Rolls for 1165. Sir Thomas Wortley, born in 1440 lived in the manor Wortley, believed to be Wortley Hall, which has subsequently been rebuilt twice. First by Sir Richard Wortley in 1586 and later by Mr Edward Wortley between 1743 and 1757, but it was not fully completed until about 1800. Today, the Hall is used as a hotel and conference venue with 57 bedrooms. The dining

rooms include original wood panelling; magnificent fireplaces and the ceilings are arguably the finest examples of Renaissance style friezes in Great Britain. The 26 acres of formal garden and woodland include a small lake, peaceful walks and an abundance of wildlife.

• Wortley Hall.

To visit the hall, proceed along the drive and follow it round to the right, but to continue the walk climb a stile on the left after 120yds, directly opposite Avenue Cottage. A grassy footpath leads up through a field with good views to the right towards Barnsley. Climb a stile at the top of the field, pass through a belt of trees, then descend a flight of steps onto Hermit Hill Lane. Turn right along this then go left just beyond Royds Cottage into Well House Lane. At Well Houses, an old farm and barn conversion complex, proceed ahead along a track that leads to a stile beside a gate and walk along the right edge of a field, with fine views to the north.

3. Cross an open section of field, with Crane Greave Farm over to the right, before continuing alongside a rustic fence to reach a stile on the right. Once over turn immediately left, passing a building known as Clappers, follow its access drive out to a lane and cross straight over on to another lane leading into the hamlet of Crane Moor Nook. Towards the end of the cottages, join an enclosed and initially paved footpath on the left that heads in a north-westerly direction between fields.

This is overhung by trees and bushes and gives welcome shade on hot, sunny days. In the spring and summer the air is filled with birdsong and butterflies flutter along as they search for nectar in the profusion of wild flowers that grow in the banks and hedges.

The path eventually runs round the left edge of a field, but where it swings right towards Toad Hole Farm, go left over a stile beside a gate and walk up the left-hand side of a grassy meadow with a wall to the left. Cross the bed of a dismantled railway to enter another field.

4. Ignore the first stile on the left, but continue to a second stile and once over follow a grassy footpath round the edge of a field with houses in Thurgoland to the left. Bear left at the end of the field, along an access drive to houses, then turn right along a road through the village. Turn left in front of the Horse & Jockey Inn and after 25yds go left again, now on a footpath that descends past Thurgoland Youth Centre and playing fields to reach the A629. Cross with care to a footpath on the opposite side and walk through the middle of a large field with good views to the left over Wharncliffe Chase.

The gritstone crags that rim the chase form the western boundary of a former medieval deer park and now act as an outdoor gymnasium for rock climbers. Archaeological finds in the area have included Bronze Age and Roman artefacts, evidence of much earlier occupation. The rare nightjar migrates here from Africa in the spring to breed, while grouse and curlew add to the avian nursery in the heather.

Continue in the same direction, down the right-hand side of a second field, and join a track that leads to buildings at Huthwaite Hall, where quite considerable renovation of outbuildings and barns has recently taken place to provide very tastefully converted and prestigious residential properties.

5. Just before reaching the buildings, go left over a stile, walk through a small pasture that usually contains a horse or two, to reach a step-stile over the far wall. Veer diagonally right on the far side, now with the main house at Huthwaite behind and to the right. At a junction with Huthwaite Lane turn left, passing Huthwaite Lodge, and follow this down to a 'T' junction with a road. Turn right here past the Bridge Inn, cross the River Don to enter Forge Lane and follow this past a series of ponds, now used by anglers, to reach Wortley Top Forge on the left.

The Wortley Ironworks, probably the oldest of its type in Yorkshire, originally comprised the Low Forge, a little further down the River Don and now derelict, and the Top Forge whose history can be traced back to the 1620's. The building that stands here today is largely 18th century and has been used for various processes, but it is best known for its high quality wrought iron railway axles and bar-iron that were produced here between 1840 and 1910. By 1912 Top Forge had closed down but Low Forge continued to produce wrought iron until 1929. Since then, this part of the Don Valley has been silent and nature has virtually taken over at Low Forge. Top Forge however, with its water wheels and old forging equipment, is now an industrial museum with open days, guided tours and demonstrations of the ancient ways of making iron. There is also a miniature railway that runs around the site during open days.

6. After visiting, continue along the road, cross the Don once more then go immediately left along a broad track, with the Don down to the left and Wortley Forge on the opposite bank. The track soon swings up and right, passes between a row of terraced cottages, various outbuildings and garages, before running along the bottom edge of a sloping field. Cross a bridge over the dismantled railway at the far end of the field to return to Cote Green Car Park on the opposite side.

• One of the tilt hammers, Top Forge.
• Wortley Mill & the River Don.
• Wortley Parish Church.

118

The Five Rise Locks, Shipley Glen & Saltaire

Hirst Wood – Leeds & Liverpool Canal – Bingley – Eldwick Hall – Shipley Glen – Saltaire

Introduction

A tremendous walk through the Aire Valley and across the southern slopes of Ilkley Moor, finishing along the rocky rim of Shipley Glenn. There is an opportunity to ride on the Shipley Glen Tramway and also visit the famous village of Saltaire and its huge mill, built by Sir Titus Salt.

Points of interest

There is so much to see and do on this walk. The Leeds & Liverpool Canal is raised by almost 60ft at Bingley by an elegant flight of five locks. The canal itself is a busy recreational waterway with many brightly painted narrow boats adding splashes of colour to the walk. The Shipley Glen Tramway has the distinction of being the oldest working cable tramway in Britain, while Saltaire is the largest and most complete model village from the 19th century.

Information

Distance & time:	8.5 miles (13.7km). 3.5 - 4 hrs not including stops.
Start & finish:	Hirst Wood (see parking).
Maps:	OS Explorer 288 Bradford & Huddersfield.
Parking:	Hirst Wood -1 mile (1.6km) along Hirst Lane from A650 Saltaire roundabout. Grid Ref: SE131382.
Public Transport:	Trains from Bradford, Bingley, Keighley and Skipton. Buses from several places including Bradford, Guiseley & Keighley. Tel: Metroline on 0113 245 7676.
Refreshments:	Pubs in Saltaire, Bingley & Shipley Glen. Café at Saltaire & Bingley.
Tourist Information:	Saltaire Tourist Information & Gift Shop, 2 Victoria Road, Saltaire Village. BD18 3LA. Tel: 01274 774993.
Shipley Glen Tramway:	For details of opening times and days - Tel: 01274 589010.

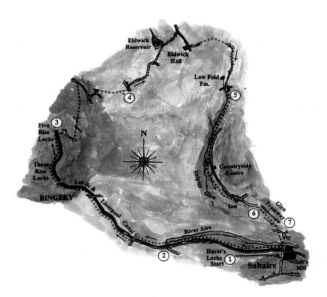

• Shipley Glen

Directions

1. From the car park, cross the swing-bridge at Hirst Locks and go left along the towpath of the Leeds & Liverpool Canal.

The canal runs through a lovely wooded section of the Aire Valley here, with bluebells, wood anemones and celandine carpeting the floor in spring, while the river babbles along down to the right. The valley creates a natural wildlife corridor between Bradford and Keighley, with numerous birds, butterflies and wildfowl making use of the diverse habitats along the way. The Leeds & Liverpool is the longest single canal in Britain and without doubt one of the country's most dramatic and varied as it passes through some of northern England's most industrialised centres, through peaceful meadows and pastures, then over the remote Pennine Hills on its journey between Yorkshire and Lancashire. The canal was started in 1770 with work beginning at both ends simultaneously, but it took 46 years before the two ends of this 127 mile long navigation could be joined by Robert Whitworth's 1,640 yard tunnel. Originally built as a trade route linking the North Sea, via the Aire & Calder navigation at Leeds, to the Irish Sea at the port of Liverpool. Little commercial traffic uses the canal today but it serves as a recreational waterway for thousands of pleasure craft and narrow boats.

The reason why the engineers decided to build the canal parallel to the river, rather than make the Aire itself navigable, probably lies in the fickle nature of the river. Following heavy rains in the Dales, the river's volume increases dramatically, sweeping all before it and flooding vast areas of low-lying land. Conversely, in dry summers it becomes little more than a shallow stream, making it totally impractical as a reliable navigation.

2. The canal eventually crosses the River Aire via a seven-arched aqueduct before reaching bridge No. 206 where it is necessary to cross to the opposite side of the canal and rejoin the towpath past Dowley Gap Locks. For those in need of refreshment, the Fisherman's Inn is just beyond here on the left, but otherwise continue alongside the canal towards Bingley.

As the canal enters Bingley, the large mill chimney of the famous Damart company can be seen on the right while the modern headquarters of the Bradford and Bingley Building Society occupy a prominent position near to the town centre.

The towpath ascends past the Bingley Three Rise Locks and then reaches the spectacular Five Rise Locks.

• A view along the Leeds & Liverpool Canal from Five Rise Locks

These were designed by John Longbotham, a canal engineer of Halifax, and built in 1774 by local stonemasons. The locks are 14ft 4in (4.4m) wide and raise and lower boats 59ft 2in (18m) over a distance of 320ft (97.5m). They hold 90,000 gallons (409,140 litres) of water and it takes approximately30 minutes for each boat to pass through. Luckily there is a small café at the top of the locks for those waiting their turn.

3. At the top of the locks, cross the swing-bridge over the canal and walk up Beck Lane, veering right at the top with a wall and allotments to the right. Just before Hall Bank Drive comes in from the right, cross the road and go left up a narrow surfaced lane with a small stream to the right. This soon joins an enclosed footpath that rises through housing developments on the outskirts of Bingley, crosses a road and continues climbing to reach another road called Pinedale. Walk up this, cross another road, then rejoin the footpath that eventually runs through woodland to reach Lady Lane. Turn right along this and continue along Dane Bank before swinging left into College Road. Alongside Lady Park Nursing Home go left into Nicholson Close, follow the road round to the right where a signposted footpath between houses climbs steps into fields. Climb a step stile over a wall, go right on the far side, now with splendid views to the right over the Pennine hills. Climb a second stile then bear diagonally left across a field, pass to the left of a ruined barn then follow the wallside footpath out to a road.

4. Turn left for 20yds then go right along a public bridleway that crosses the high point of this walk. 80yds beyond a sharp right-hand bend, turn left along a partly paved footpath that descends initially to cross stepping stones over Loadpit Beck before ascending beneath the retaining earth bank of Eldwick Reservoir. At a junction with a road turn right, but immediately alongside the buildings of Eldwick Hall, cross the road, with care, onto an enclosed track between fields. Where the track enters a field proceed ahead alongside a wall and into a second field to reach a wall corner and

footpath sign. Turn right here across the centre of the field on a footpath that forms part of the Dales Way Link. Pass to the rear of Goldcar Farm, then turn right along its access drive to reach Bingley Road. Cross this to join a continuation footpath on the opposite side that swings round to the right of a barn. The footpath now runs along the left bank of a lovely little glen, with Loadpit Beck babbling away in the bottom, birds singing from the overhanging boughs and wildflowers adorning the banks.

• The New Mill, Saltaire

5. This is the infant Shipley Glen, which soon becomes much deeper with gritstone outcrops along its rim, forming a natural playground for rock climbers who test their skills on the ripples, creases and cracks of these sedimentary deposits. The Glen has long been a popular weekend and bank holiday venue for the people of Bradford and surrounding towns who come to stroll, play ball games, fly kites, horse ride or simply spread out a picnic blanket and enjoy an alfresco meal.

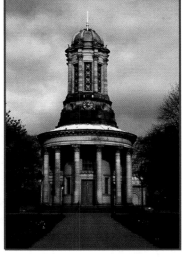

Continue along any of the worn paths that cross the strip of grassland between Glen Road on the left and Shipley Glen to the right until you reach the Old Glen Public House. However, it is well worth dropping in at Brackenhall Countryside Centre, part way along Glen Road, where you can find out more about the wildlife and geology of the area. Now walk down Prod Lane to its end by a small amusement area.

6. Towards the end of the 19th century, Shipley Glen was owned by a Colonel Maude, who developed the area into a small tourist attraction by building several fair ground rides, pleasure gardens and amusements. In its heyday, as many as 17,000 people would flock from the local towns to enjoy the attractions and breathe fresh Pennine air.

At this point you have a choice. Either follow the surfaced footpath that descends gently through the trees or, as a pleasant alternative, take a short ride on the Shipley Glen Tramway.

This was built by a local entrepreneur Sam Wilson and opened on 18th May 1895. The Tramway has a gauge of 20 inches along two tracks with a pair of Toastrack tramcars on each line and a maximum gradient of 1 in 7. It has the distinction of being the oldest cable tramway in Britain and runs up and down a near quarter mile track through scenic woodland. At the bottom of the ride is a replica Edwardian shop both displaying and vending pure nostalgia. There is also a small museum which is open most weekends, as is the Tramway.

• The Church, Saltaire.
• Shipley Glen Tramway.

7. At the bottom of the hill walk along the right edge of playing fields, cross a road and go left for a few yards before entering Roberts Park, formerly Saltaire Park and opened in 1871.

It was landscaped by William Gay of Bradford and contains mature specimen trees, flower borders, playing fields a cricket pitch and a statue of Sir Titus Salt.

Walk along the left edge of the park, cross a footbridge spanning the River Aire then cross the canal bridge alongside New Mill to enter Saltaire.

Saltaire is the largest and most intact model village built in the 19th century and is of great local and national importance. It was the brainchild of Sir Titus Salt, a self-made and highly successful Victorian wool merchant. The village was built between 1851 and 1876 to replace four existing factories and provided employment, living accommodation, shops, schools, churches, a library, meeting halls and recreational space in an attempt to improve living conditions at the time. The area suffered economic depression, with the decline of the textile industry and in 1986 Salt's Mill closed after almost 133 years. It was designated a conservation area in 1971 and since 1986 a programme of restoration and regeneration work has been carried out by public and private sectors. The mill, built in the Venetian Gothic style, once employed 2,500 workers.

After visiting, retrace your steps to the canal and go left along the towpath back to Hirst Locks.

• Salt's Mill